Berlitz®

Polish

phrase book &

PTTK
USTRZYKI
DOLNE

BACÓWKA PTTK 15 min.
POD MAŁĄ RAWKĄ

POŁONINA
CARYŃSKA
PRZEŁĘCZ
WYZNIAŃSKA

1h

PTTK
DOLNE

5 min

Berlitz Publishing
New York London Singapore

Contacting the Editors
Every effort has been made to provide accurate information in this publication, but changes are inevitable. The publisher cannot be responsible for any resulting loss, inconvenience or injury. We would appreciate it if readers would call our attention to any errors or outdated information. We also welcome your suggestions; if you come across a relevant expression not in our phrase book, please contact us at: **comments@berlitzpublishing.com**

All Rights Reserved
© 2018 Apa Digital (CH) AG and Apa Publications (UK) Ltd.
Berlitz Trademark Reg. U.S. Patent Office and other countries. Marca Registrada. Used under license from Berlitz Investment Corporation.

Thirteenth Printing: August 2018
Printed in China

Editor: Helen Fanthorpe
Translation: updated by Wordbank
Cover Design: Rebeka Davies
Interior Design: Beverley Speight
Picture Researcher: Tom Smyth
Cover Photos: all iStock

Interior Photos: Kevin Cummins/APA 41, 48; iStockphoto 141,144,151, 152; 156, 165; Britta Jaschinski/APA 12, 37, 44; Lucy Johnston/APA 178; Jon Santa Cruz/APA 124,148; Corrie Wingate/APA 19, 24, 30, 65, 70, 81, 86, 100, 103, 110, 115, 117, 122, 130, 162; Gregory Wrona/APA 1, 15, 54, 56, 76, 96, 107, 129, 132,137, 138, 142, 146.

Distribution

UK, Ireland and Europe
Apa Publications (UK) Ltd
sales@insightguides.com
United States and Canada
Ingram Publisher Services
ips@ingramcontent.com
Australia and New Zealand
Woodslane
info@woodslane.com.au
Southeast Asia
Apa Publications (SN) Pte
singaporeoffice@insightguides.com

Worldwide
Apa Publications (UK) Ltd
sales@insightguides.com

Special Sales, Content Licensing, and CoPublishing
Discounts available for bulk quantities. We can create special editions, personalized jackets, and corporate imprints. sales@insightguides.com; www.insightguides.biz

Contents

Food & Drink

People

In an Emergency

Dictionary

Pronunciation

This section is designed to familiarize you with the sounds of Polish using our simplified phonetic transcription. You'll find the pronunciation of the Polish letters and sounds explained below, together with their imitated equivalents. To use this system, found throughout the phrase book, simply read the pronunciation as if it were English, noting any special rules below. Underlined letters indicate that the syllable should be stressed. In Polish, stress falls on the penultimate syllable: *autobus*, *szkoła*. In some words of foreign origin (mostly Latin and Greek), stress is assigned to the third syllable from the end of the word: *uniwersytet*.

Consonants/Consonant Clusters

Letter	Approximate Pronunciation	Symbol	Example	Pronunciation
c	like ts in fits	ts	cały	*tsah-wyh*
ć, ci	a soft, very short version of chee in cheese	ch'	cień	*ch'yen'*
cz	like ch in church but harder	ch	czapka	*chahp-kah*
dz	like ds in beds	dz	dzwonek	*dzvoh-nehk*
drz, dż	like j in jam	dj	drzwi	*djvee*
dź, dzi	like ge in genius	dj'	dzień	*dj'yen'*
h, ch	hard, like the ch in Scottish loch	h	chleb	*hlehp*
j	like y in yes	y	jutro	*yoo-troh*
ł	like w in win	w	łóżko	*woozh-koh*
ń, ni	like ni in onion	n'	nie	*n'yeh*

r	rolled, distinct at the end of words	r	**rower**	_roh-vehr_
sz	like sh in shot but harder	**sh**	**szkoła**	_shkoh-wah_
ś, si	soft, very short version of shee in sheep	**sh'**	**śmieci**	_sh'myeh-ch'ee_
w	like v in very	**v**	**woda**	_voh-dah_
ź, zi	like s in pleasure but softer	**zh'**	**źródło**	_zh'rood-woh_
ż, rz	like s in pleasure but harder	**zh**	**żaba**	_zhah-bah_

Letters b, d, f, k, l, m, n, p, s, t, z are pronounced approximately as in English.
* The apostrophe (') in phonetics indicates a softening of the sound.

Polish is a Slavic language and is the mother tongue of 99% of the population in Poland. While many people speak English in the major cities, in the countryside, communication difficulties are to be expected. Overall, knowing some Polish will come in use.

Polish is a phonetic language, meaning that there is a good correlation of sound to spelling - and its pronunciation is much more systematic than that of English.

Vowels

Letter	Approximate Pronunciation	Symbol	Example	Pronunciation
a	like a in father	**ah**	**dach**	*dahh*
e	like e in ten	**eh**	**bez**	*behs*
i	like ee in keen	**ee**	**kino**	*kee-noh*
o	like o in so	**oh**	**okno**	*ohk-noh*
u, ó	like u in put	**oo**	**sufit**	*soo-feet*
y	like i in fit	**yh**	**buty**	*boo-tyh*
ą	1. nasal, like an in fiancé, at the end of a word	**1. ohm**	**1. są**	*1. sohm*
	2. pronounced ohn before a consonant	**2. ohn**	**2. kąt**	*2. kohnt*
	3. pronounced ohm before b and p	**3. ohm**	**3. ząb**	*3. zohmb*
ę	1. ehn before a consonant	**1. ehn**	**1. ręka**	*1. rehn-kah*
	2. ehm before b and p	**2. ehm**	**2. kępa**	*2. kehm-pah*
	3. eh when final in a word	**3. eh**	**3. tę**	*3. teh*

How to use this Book

Sometimes you see two alternatives in italics, separated by a slash. Choose the one that's right for your situation.

ESSENTIAL

I'm here on vacation [holiday]/business.

Przyjechałem m **/Przyjechałam** f **tutaj na wakacje/służbowo.** *pshyh•yeh•hah•wehm/ pshyh•yeh•hah•wahm tuh•tahy nah vah•kahts•yeh/ swuhzh•boh•voh*

I'm going to…
I'm staying at the… Hotel.

Jadę do… *yah•deh doh…*
Zatrzymałem m **/Zatrzymałam** f **się w Hotelu…** *zah•tshyh•mah•wehm/ zah•tshyh•mah•wahm sh'yeh fhoh•teh•luh…*

Words you may see are shown in YOU MAY SEE boxes.

YOU MAY SEE…

ŁODZIE RATUNKOWE	life boats
KAPOKI	life jackets
POKŁAD	deck

Any of the words or phrases listed can be plugged into the sentence below.

Tickets

When's…to Cracow?

O której jest…do Krakowa? *oh ktuh•rehy yehst…doh krah•koh•vah*

the (first) bus	**(pierwszy) autobus**	*(pyehr•shyh) ahw•toh•buhs*
the (next) flight	**(następny) samolot**	*(nahs•tehm•pnyh) sah•moh•loht*
the (last) train	**(ostatni) pociąg**	*(ohs•taht•n'ee) poh•ch'yonk*

Polish phrases appear in purple.

Read the simplified pronunciation as if it were English. For more on pronunciation, see page 7.

At the Bank

I'd like to change money.

Chciałbym *m* **/Chciałabym** *f* **wymienić pieniądze.** *hfh'yahw•byhm/hfh'yah•wah•byhm vyh•myeh•n'eech' pyeh•n'yohn•dzeh*

What's the exchange rate?

Jaki jest kurs wymiany? *yah•kee yehst kurs vyh•myah•nyh*

How much is the fee?
For Numbers, see page 171.

Jaka jest prowizja? *yah•kah yest proh•veez•yah*

Related phrases can be found by going to the page number indicated.

When different gender forms apply, the masculine form is followed by *m*; feminine by *f*

When addressing a man in a formal situation, use **pan** (sir); when addressing a woman, use **pani** (ma'am or madam). Throughout this phrase book **pan** is used for the sake of simplicity. When speaking to a woman, be sure to substitute **pani** for **pan**.

Information boxes contain relevant country, culture and language tips.

Expressions you may hear are shown in You May Hear boxes.

YOU MAY HEAR...

Bilet/Paszport, proszę.
bee•leht/pahsh•pohrt proh•sheh

Your ticket/passport, please.

Color-coded side bars identify each section of the book.

Survival

Arrival & Departure

ESSENTIAL

I'm here on vacation/business.	**Przyjechałem** *m* /**Przyjechałam** *f* **tutaj na wakacje/łużbowo.** *pshyh·yeh·<u>hah</u>·wehm/pshyh·yeh·<u>hah</u>·wahm <u>too</u>·tahy nah vah·<u>kahts</u>·yeh/swoozh·<u>boh</u>·voh*
I'm going to...	**Jadę do...** *<u>yah</u>·deh doh...*
I'm staying at the... Hotel.	**Zatrzymałem** *m* /**Zatrzymałam** *f* **się w Hotelu...** *zah·tshyh·<u>mah</u>·wehm/zah·tshyh·<u>mah</u>·wahm sh'yeh fhoh·<u>teh</u>·loo...*

YOU MAY HEAR...

Bilet/Paszport, proszę. *<u>bee</u>·leht/<u>pahsh</u>·pohrt <u>proh</u>·sheh*	Your ticket/passport, please.
Jaki jest cel pana wizyty? *<u>yah</u>·kee yehst tsehl <u>pah</u>·nah vee·<u>zyh</u>·tyh*	What's the purpose of your visit?
Gdzie pan się zatrzymał? *gdj'yeh pahn sh'yeh zah·<u>tshyh</u>·mahw*	Where are you staying?
Jak długo pan tu będzie? *yahk <u>dwoo</u>·goh pahn too <u>behn</u>·dj'ye*	How long are you staying?
Z kim pan tutaj jest? *skeem pahn <u>too</u>·tahy yehst*	Who are you here with?

When addressing a man in a formal situation, use **pan** (sir);
when addressing a woman, use **pani** (ma'am or madam).
Throughout this phrase book **pan** is used for the sake of simplicity.
When speaking to a woman, be sure to substitute **pani** for **pan**.

Border Control

I'm just passing through.	**Jestem tu tylko przejazdem.** *yeh•stehm too tyhl•koh psheh•yahz•dehm*
I would like to declare…	**Chciałbym** *m* /**Chciałabym** *f* **zadeklarować…** *hch'yahw•byhm/hch'yah•wah•byhm zah•dehk•lah•roh•vahch'…*
I have nothing to declare.	**Nie mam nic do oclenia.** *n'yeh mahm n'eets doh ohts•leh•n'yah*

YOU MAY HEAR…

Czy ma pan coś do oclenia? *chyh mah pahn tsohsh' doh ohts•leh•n'yah*

Anything to declare?

Musi pan zapłacić za to cło. *moo•sh'ee pahn zah•pwa•ch'eech' zah toh tswoh*

You must pay duty on this.

Proszę otworzyć torbę/walizkę. *proh•sheh oht•foh•zhyhch' tohr•beh/vah•lees•keh*

Please open your bag/suitcase.

YOU MAY SEE…

ODPRAWA CELNA	customs
TOWARY BEZCŁOWE	duty-free goods
TOWARY DO OCLENIA	goods to declare
NIC DO OCLENIA	nothing to declare
KONTROLA PASZPORTOWA	passport control
POLICJA	police
DLA PERSONELU	staff only

Biura linii lotniczych
Airline offices

→

Punkt spotkań
Meeting point

Money

ESSENTIAL

Where's...?	**Gdzie jest...?** *gdj'yeh yehst...*
the ATM	**bankomat** *bahn•koh•maht*
the bank	**bank** *bahnk*
the currency exchange office	**kantor** *kahn•tohr*
When does the bank open/close?	**O której otwierają/zamykają bank?** *oh ktoo•rehy oht•fyeh•rah•yohm/zah•myh•kah•yohm bahnk*
I'd like to change dollars/pounds into zlotys.	**Chciałbym** *m* **/Chciałabym** *f* **wymienić dolary/ funty na złotówki.** *hch'yahw•byhm/ hch'yah•wah•byhm vyh•myeh•n'eech do•lah•ryh/ foon•tyh nah zwoh•toof•kee*
I want to cash some travelers checks.	**Chcę zrealizować czeki podróżne.** *htseh zreh•ah•lee•zoh•vahch' cheh•kee pohd•roozh•neh*

Prices in Poland generally include **VAT** (sales tax). The price you will pay is the price provided on the sales tag.

At the Bank

I'd like to change money.	**Chciałbym** m /**Chciałabym** f **wymienić pieniądze.** _hch'yahw•byhm/hch'yah•wah•byhm vyh•myeh•n'eech' pyeh•n'yohn•dzeh_
What's the exchange rate?	**Jaki jest kurs wymiany?** _yah•kee yehst koors vyh•myah•nyh_
How much is the fee?	**Jaka jest prowizja?** _yah•kah yest proh•veez•yah_
I've lost my travelers checks/ credit cards.	**Zgubiłem** m /**Zgubiłam** f **czeki podróżne/karty kredytowe.** _zgoo•bee•wehm/zgoo•bee•wahm cheh•kee pohd•roozh•neh/kahr•tyh kreh•dyh•toh•veh_
My card was stolen.	**Ukradli mi kartę.** _oo•krahd•lee mee kahr•teh_
My card doesn't work.	**Moja karta nie działa.** _moh•yah kahr•tah n'yeh dj'yah•wah_

For Numbers, see page 171.

YOU MAY SEE...

Polish currency is currently the **złoty**; one **złoty** is made up of 100 **groszy**. Soon Poland may adopt the euro as its national currency; until then **złoty** is the accepted form of payment.
Coins: 1, 2, 5, 10, 20, 50 **groszy**; 1, 2, 5 **złoty**.
Bills: 10, 20, 50, 100, 200 **złoty**.

YOU MAY SEE...

WŁÓŻ KARTĘ	insert credit card
WYBIERZ JĘZYK	select language
WPROWADŹ PIN	enter your PIN
WCIŚNIJ KLAWISZ	press key
WYPŁATA GOTÓWKI	cash withdrawal
INNA KWOTA	different amount
STAN RACHUNKU	balance inquiry
WOLNE ŚRODKI	available balance
AKCEPTUJ	enter
ANULUJ	cancel
POPRAW	clear
KONTYNUUJ	next
KONIEC	end
POTWIERDZENIE	receipt

17

Banks are usually open between 8:00 a.m. and 6:00 p.m. When changing cash and travelers checks, you will need to show your passport. Numerous **kantory** (currency exchange offices) provide exchange services and usually have a better exchange rate than banks. Some large hotels will exchange cash and travelers checks for their guests. In cities and larger towns you'll find **bankomaty**, ATMs that accept various international bank and credit cards. Travelers checks are not currently accepted in stores and hotels.

Getting Around

ESSENTIAL

How do I get to town?	**Jak stąd dojechać do miasta?** *yahk stohnt doh·yeh·hahch' doh myahs·tah*
Where's...?	**Gdzie jest...?** *gdj'yeh yehst...*
the airport	*lotnisko loht·n'ees·koh*
the train [railway] station	**dworzec kolejowy** *dvoh·zhehts koh·leh·yoh·vyh*
the bus station	**dworzec autobusowy** *dvoh·zhehts ahw·toh·boo·soh·vyh*
the metro [underground] station	**stacja metra** *stahts·yah meht·rah*
Is it far from here?	**Czy to daleko stąd?** *chyh toh dah·leh·koh stohnt*
Where can I buy tickets?	**Gdzie mogę kupić bilety?** *gdj'yeh moh·geh koo·peech' bee·leh·tyh*
A one-way [single]/ round-trip [return] ticket to...	**Bilet w jedną stonę/powrotny do...** *bee·leht vyehd·nohm stroh·neh/pohv·roht·nyh doh...*
Are there any discounts?	**Czy są jakieś zniżki?** *chyh sohm yah·kyehsh' zn'eesh·kee*
Where can I get a taxi?	**Gdzie mogę złapać taksówkę?** *gdj'yeh moh·geh zwah·pahch' tahk·soof·keh*
Please take me to this address.	**Proszę mnie zawieźć pod ten adres.** *proh·sheh mn'yeh zah·vyehsh'ch' poht tehn ahd·rehs*
Where can I rent a car?	**Gdzie mogę wynająć samochód?** *gdj'yeh moh·geh vyh·nah·yohn'ch' sah·moh·hoot*
Can I have a map, please?	**Poproszę mapę.** *poh·proh·sheh mah·peh*

Tickets

When's…to Cracow?	**O której jest…do Krakowa?** *oh ktoo·rehy yehst… doh krah·koh·vah*
the (first) bus	**(pierwszy) autobus** *(pyehr·shyh) ahw·toh·boos*
the (next) flight	**(następny) samolot** *(nahs·tehm·pnyh) sah·moh·loht*
the (last) train	**(ostatni) pociąg** *(ohs·taht·n'ee) poh·ch'yonk*
Where can I buy a ticket?	**Gdzie mogę kupić bilet?** *gdj'yeh moh·geh koo·peech' bee·leht*
One/two ticket(s), please.	**Jeden bilet/Dwa bilety proszę.** *yeh·dehn bee·leht/ dvah bee·leh·tyh proh·sheh*
A…ticket.	**Bilet…** *bee·leht…*
one-way [single]	**w jedną stronę** *vyehd·nohm stroh·neh*
round-trip [return]	**powrotny** *pohv·roht·nyh*
first class	**w pierwszej klasie** *fpyehr·shehy klah·sh'yeh*
economy class	**w klasie turystycznej** *fklah·sh'yeh too·ryhs·tyhch·nehy*
How much?	**Ile to kosztuje?** *ee·leh toh kohsh·too·yeh*
Is there a discount for…?	**Czy jest zniżka dla…?** *chyh yehst zn'eesh·kah dlah…*
children	**dzieci** *dj'ye·ch'ee*
students	**studentów** *stoo·dehn·toof*
senior citizens	**emerytów** *eh·meh·ryh·toof*

I have an e-ticket.	**Mam bilet elektroniczny.** *mahm bee•leht eh•lehk•troh•neech•nyh*
Can I buy a ticket on the bus/train?	**Czy można kupić bilet w autobusie/pociągu?** *chyh mohzh•nah koo•peech' bee•leht v ahw•toh•boo•sh'yeh/poh•ch'yohn•goo*
I'd like to...my reservation.	**Chciałbym m /Chciałabym f...moją rezerwację.** *hch'yahw•byhm/hch'yah•wah•byhm...moh•yohm reh•zehr•vahts•yeh*
cancel	**odwołać** *ohd•voh•wahch'*
change	**zmienić** *zmyeh•n'eech'*
confirm	**potwierdzić** *poh•tfyehr•dj'eech'*

Plane

Airport Transfer

How much is a taxi to the airport?	**Ile kosztuje taksówka na lotnisko?** *ee•leh kohsh•too•yeh tahk•soof•kah nah loht•n'ees•koh*
To...Airport, please.	**Na lotnisko...proszę.** *nah loht•n'ees•koh...proh•sheh*
My airline is...	**Lecę liniami...** *leh•tseh lee•n'yah•mee...*
My flight leaves at...	**Mam samolot o...** *mahm sah•moh•loht oh...*
I'm in a hurry.	**Spieszę się.** *spyeh•sheh sh'yeh*
Can you drive faster/slower?	**Mógłby pan jechać szybciej/wolniej?** *moogw•byh pahn yeh•hahch' shyhp•ch'yehy/vohl•n'yehy*

For Time, see page 173.

YOU MAY HEAR...

Jakimi liniami pan leci? *yah•kee•mee lee•n'yah•mee pahn leh•ch'ee*	What airline are you flying?
Lot krajowy czy zagraniczny? *loht krah•yoh•wyh chyh zah•grah•n'eech•nyh*	Domestic or international flight?
Który terminal? *ktoo•ryh tehr•mee•nahl*	What terminal?

YOU MAY SEE...

PRZYLOTY	arrivals
ODLOTY	departures
ODBIÓR BAGAŻU	baggage claim
ODLOTY KRAJOWE	domestic flights
ODLOTY MIĘDZYNARODOWE	international flights
STANOWISKO ODPRAWY	check-in
WYJŚCIA	departure gates
NIC DO OCLENIA	nothing to declare
TOWARY DO OCLENIA	goods to declare
INFORMACJA CELNA	customs information
WOLNY OBSZAR CELNY	duty-free zone

Checking In

Where's check-in?	**Gdzie jest stanowisko odprawy?** *gdj'yeh yehst stah•noh•vees•koh oht•prah•vyh*
My name is...	**Nazywam się...** *nah•zyh•vahm sh'yeh...*
I'm going to...	**Lecę do...** *leh•tseh doh...*
How much luggage is allowed?	**Ile bagażu mogę wziąć?** *ee•leh bah•gah•zhoo moh•geh wzh'yohn'ch'*
Which terminal does flight...leave from?	**Z którego terminalu odlatuje lot numer...?** *sktoo•reh•goh tehr•mee•nah•loo ohd•lah•too•yeh loht noo•mehr...*
Which gate does flight...leave from?	**Które wyjście jest dla lotu numer...?** *ktoo•reh vyhy•sh'ch'yeh yehst dlah loh•too noo•mehr...*
I'd like a window/ an aisle seat.	**Chciałbym m /Chciałabym f miejsce przy oknie/ przejściu.** *hch'yahw•byhm/hch'yah•wah•byhm myehys•tseh pshyh ohk•n'yeh/pshehy•sh'ch'yoo*

Can I take this on board?	**Czy mogę to wziąć jako bagaż podręczny?** *chyh moh•geh toh vzh'yohn'ch' yah•koh bah•gahsh pohd•rehn•chnyh*
When do we leave/arrive?	**O której startujemy/lądujemy?** *oh ktoo•rehy stahr•too•yeh•myh/lohn•doo•yeh•myh*
Is flight…delayed?	**Czy lot…jest opóźniony?** *chyh loht… yehst oh•poozh'•n'yoh•nyh*
How late will it be?	**O ile jest opóźniony?** *oh ee•leh yehst oh•poozh'•n'yoh•nyh*

YOU MAY HEAR…

Proszę następną osobę! *proh•sheh nah•stehmp•nohm oh•soh•beh*	Next person, please!
Poproszę paszport/bilet. *poh•proh•sheh pahsh•pohrt/bee•leht*	Your passport/ticket, please.
Ma pan jakiś bagaż do nadania? *mah pahn yah•keesh' bah•gahsh doh nah•dah•n'yah*	Are you checking in any luggage?
Ma pan nadbagaż. *mah pahn nahd•bah•gash*	You have excess luggage.
Czy pan się sam pakował? *chyh pahn sh'yeh sahm pah•koh•vahw*	Did you pack these bags yourself?
Proszę opróżnić kieszenie. *proh•sheh ohp•roozh•n'eech' kyeh•sheh•n'yeh*	Please empty your pockets.
Proszę zdjąć buty. *proh•sheh zdyohn'ch' boo•tyh*	Please take off your shoes.
Zapraszamy pasażerów na pokład samolotu do…, rejs numer… *zah•prah•shah•myh pah•sah•zheh•roov nah pohk•wahd sah•moh•loh•too doh… rehys noo•mehr…*	Now boarding flight number…to…

Luggage

Where is/are…?	**Gdzie jest/są…?** *gdj'yeh yehst/sohm…*
the luggage carts [trolleys]	**wózki bagażowe** <u>voos</u>•kee bah•gah•<u>zhoh</u>•veh
luggage lockers/ baggage room	**skrytki bagażowe/przechowalnia bagażu** <u>skryht</u>•kee bah•gah•<u>zhoh</u>•veh/psheh•hoh•<u>vahl</u>•n'yah bah•<u>gah</u>•zhoo
the baggage claim	**odbiór bagażu** <u>ohd</u>•byoor bah•<u>gah</u>•zhoo
My luggage has been lost.	**Zgubili mój bagaż.** zgoo•<u>bee</u>•lee mooy <u>bah</u>•gahsh
My baggage has been stolen.	**Ukradli mi bagaż.** oo•<u>krahd</u>•lee mee <u>bah</u>•gahsh
My suitcase was damaged.	**Moja walizka została uszkodzona.** <u>moh</u>•yah vah•<u>lees</u>•kah zohs•<u>tah</u>•wah oosh•koh•<u>dzoh</u>•nah

Finding your Way

Where is/are…?	**Gdzie jest/są…?** *gdj'yeh yehst/sohm…*
the currency exchange office	**kantor** <u>kahn</u>•tohr
the exit	**wyjście** <u>vyhsh</u>'ch'yeh
the taxis	**taksówki** tahk•<u>soof</u>•kee
Where is the car rental [hire]?	**Gdzie można wynająć samochód?** gdj'yeh <u>mohzh</u>•nah wyh•<u>nah</u>•yohnch' sah•<u>moh</u>•hoot
Is there…into town?	**Czy można stąd dojechać…do centrum?** chyh <u>mohzh</u>•nah stohnt doh•<u>yeh</u>•hahch'…doh <u>tsehn</u>•troom
a bus	**autobusem** ahw•toh•<u>boo</u>•sehm
a train	**pociągiem** poh•<u>ch'yohn</u>•gyehm
a metro	**metrem** <u>meht</u>•rehm

For Asking Directions, see page 34.

Train

Where's the train station?	**Gdzie jest dworzec kolejowy?** *gdj'yeh yehst <u>dvoh</u>•zhehts koh•leh•<u>yoh</u>•vyh*
Is it far from here?	**Czy to daleko stąd?** *chyh toh dah•<u>leh</u>•koh stohnt*
Where is/are...?	**Gdzie jest/są...?** *gdj'yeh yehst/sohm...*
the ticket office	**kasa biletowa** *<u>kah</u>•sah bee•leh•<u>toh</u>•vah*

Poland has a well-developed train network operated by state-owned **PKP (Polskie Koleje Państwowe)** and some regional operators (e.g. **Tanie Linie Kolejowe, TLK**, and **Koleje Mazowieckie, KM**). Train travel within Poland is relatively cheap. Fares differ according to the route, type of train and seating class you select. Trains that require seat reservations display the letter **R** on both the schedule and the car. You can buy tickets at the train station's ticket office or at an Orbis travel agency. It is also possible to buy tickets on the train for an additional fee. Tickets for **InterCity,** express trains and **TLK** trains are also available on the internet (www.pkp.pl). If you need a reservation, your ticket will be automatically sold with **miejscówka**, the reservation component, subject to extra charge.

YOU MAY SEE…

PERONY	platforms
INFORMACJA	information
REZERWACJE	reservations
PRZYJAZDY	arrivals
ODJAZDY	departures
KASA BILETOWA (CZYNNA/ NIECZYNNA)	ticket office (open/closed)
ROZKŁAD JAZDY	schedule [timetable]
WYJŚCIE (EWAKUACYJNE)	(emergency) exit
TOALETY	restroom [toilet]
POSTÓJ TAKSÓWEK	taxi stand
BIURO RZECZY ZNALEZIONYCH	lost-and-found [lost property office]

the information desk	**informacja** een·fohr·*mah*·tsyah
luggage lockers/ baggage room	**skrytki bagażowe/przechowalnia bagażu** *skryht*·kee bah·gah·*zhoh*·veh/psheh·hoh·*vahl*·n'yah bah·*gah*·zhoo
the platforms	**perony** peh·*roh*·nyh
Can I have a schedule [timetable]?	**Czy mogę prosić rozkład jazdy?** chyh *moh*·geh *proh*·sh'eech' *rohs*·kwaht *yahz*·dyh
How long is the trip [journey]?	**Jak długo trwa podróż?** yahk *dwoo*·goh trfah *poh*·droosh
Do I have to change trains?	**Czy muszę się przesiadać?** chyh *moo*·sheh sh'yeh psheh·*sh'yah*·dahch'
Do I need a reservation for this train?	**Muszę kupować miejscówkę?** *moo*·sheh koo·*poh*·vahch' myehys·*tsoof*·keh

For Asking Directions, see page 34.

For Tickets, see page 19.

Departures

Which track [platform] does the train to... leave from?	**Z którego toru [peronu] odjeżdża pociąg do...?** *sktoo-reh-goh toh-roo [peh-roh-noo] ohd-yehzh-djah poh-ch'yohnk doh...*
Is this the right track [platform] for...?	**Czy to z tego toru [peronu] odjeżdża pociąg do...?** *chyh toh steh-goh toh-roo [peh-roh-noo] ohd-yehzh-djah poh-ch'yohnk doh...*
Where is track [platform]...?	**Gdzie jest tor [peron]...?** *gdj'yeh yehst tohr [peh-rohn]...*
Where do I change for...?	**Gdzie mam się przesiąść na pociąg do...?** *gdj'yeh mahm sh'yeh psheh-sh'yohn'sh'ch' nah poh-ch'yonk doh...*

On Board

Is this seat free?	**Czy to miejsce jest wolne?** *chyh toh myehys-tseh yehst vohl-neh*
That's my seat.	**To moje miejsce.** *toh moh-yeh myehys-tseh*

Bus

Where's the bus station?	**Gdzie jest dworzec autobusowy?** *gdj'yeh yehst dvoh-zhehts ahw-toh-boo-soh-vyh*

YOU MAY HEAR...

Proszę wsiadać! *proh-sheh fsh'yah-dahch'*	All aboard!
Proszę bilety do kontroli. *proh-sheh bee-leh-tyh doh kohn-troh-lee*	Tickets, please.
Następna stacja... *nahs-tehmp-nah stahts-yah...*	Next stop...
Musi pan się przesiąść w... *moo-sh'ee pahn sh'yeh psheh-sh'yohn'sh'ch' v...*	You have to change at...

Bus service in Poland is extensive. **PKS (Przedsiębiorstwo Komunikacji Samochodowej)** offers the widest range of routes; **Polski Express** also has numerous national routes. You can buy tickets for **PKS** buses at the bus station ticket office or from the driver. Tickets for **Polski Express** buses can be bought at bus stations or at special ticket offices in towns.

Is it far from here?	**Czy to daleko stąd?** *chyh toh dah·leh·koh stohnt*
How do I get to…?	**Jak dojechać do…?** *yahk doh·yeh·hahch' doh…*
Does this bus stop at…?	**Czy ten autobus zatrzymuje się w…?** *chyh tehn ahw·toh·boos zah·tshyh·moo·yeh sh'yeh v…*
Could you tell me when to get off?	**Czy może mi pan powiedzieć, kiedy wysiąść?** *chyh moh·zhe mee pahn poh·vyeh·dj'yehch' kyeh·dyh vyh·sh'on'sh'ch'*
Do I have to change buses?	**Czy muszę się przesiadać?** *chyh moo·sheh sh'yeh psheh·sh'yah·dahch'*
Stop here, please!	**Proszę się zatrzymać!** *proh·sheh sh'yeh zaht·shyh·mahch'*

For Tickets, see page 19.

For Tickets, see page 19.

YOU MAY SEE…

PRZYSTANEK AUTOBUSOWY	bus stop
OTWIERANIE DRZWI PRZYCISKIEM	press to open door
SKASUJ BILET	validate your ticket
HAMULEC BEZPIECZEŃSTWA	emergency brake
KASOWNIK	validation machine
WYJŚCIE AWARYJNE	emergency exit

Warsaw is the only Polish city with a metro service. The line passes through **Centrum** (the city center), where visitors can admire **Pałac Kultury i Nauki** (Palace of Culture and Science). Maps are located throughout metro stations and inside trains. Above-ground **tramwaje** (trams) can be found in Warsaw, Gdańsk, Poznań and many other cities.

Metro

Where's the nearest metro [underground] station?	**Gdzie jest najbliższa stacja metra?** gdj'yeh yehst nahy•bleesh•shah stahts•yah meht•rah
Where can I find a metro map?	**Gdzie mogę znaleźć mapę metra?** gdj'yeh moh•geh znah•lesh'ch' mah•peh meht•rah
Which metro goes in the direction of…?	**Które metro jedzie w stronę…?** ktoo•reh meht•roh yeh•dj'yeh fstroh•neh…
Do I have to transfer [change]?	**Czy muszę się przesiadać?** chyh moo•sheh sh'yeh psheh•sh'yah•dahch'
Is this the metro / train to…?	**Czy to metro jedzie do…?** chyh toh meht•roh yeh•dj'yeh doh…
Where are we?	**Gdzie jesteśmy?** gdj'yeh yehs•tehsh'•myh

For Tickets, see page 19.

Boat & Ferry

When is the ferry to…?	**Kiedy odpływa prom do…?** kyeh•dyh oht•pwyh•vah prohm doh…
Can I take my car?	**Czy mogę zabrać na pokład mój samochód?** chyh moh•geh zahb•rahch' nah pohk•wahd mooy sah•moh•hoot
What time is the next sailing?	**O której jest następny rejs?** oh ktoo•rehy yehst nahs•tehm•pnyh reyhs

Tickets for the metro and trams should be bought before boarding from kiosks or local shops. On boarding you must validate your ticket in a **kasownik** (validation machine). Unvalidated tickets result in an on-the-spot fine. Different types of tickets are used in different cities, but usually single-trip tickets and multiple-trip travelcards are available. In some cities electronic cards are available as well.

YOU MAY SEE...

ŁODZIE RATUNKOWE	life boats
KAPOKI	life jackets
POKŁAD	deck

Can I book a seat/ cabin?	**Chciałbym m / Chciałabym f zarezerwować miejsce siedzące/kabinę.** _hch'yahw•byhm/ hch'yah•wah•byhm zah•reh•zehr•voh•vach' myehys•tseh sh'yeh•dzohn•tse/kah•bee•neh_
How long is the crossing?	**Jak długo trwa przeprawa?** _yahk dwoo•goh trfah psheh•prah•vah_

For Tickets, see page 19.

Regular ferry services to and from Denmark and Sweden operate from Świnoujście, Gdańsk and Gdynia. There are several ferry operators who offer various cruises on the Baltic Sea on different days of the week.

Taxi

Where can I get a taxi?	**Gdzie mogę złapać taksówkę?** *gdj'yeh moh•geh zwah•pahch' tahk•soof•keh*
I'd like a taxi now/for tomorrow at…	**Chciałbym** *m* **/Chciałabym** *f* **zamówić taksówkę na jak najszybciej/na jutro na godzinę…** *hch'yahw•byhm/hch'yah•wah•byhm zah•moo•veech' tahk•soof•keh nah yahk nahy•shyhp•ch'yehy/nah yoot•roh nah goh•dj'ee•neh…*
The pick-up address is…	**Proszę mnie odebrać z…** *proh•sheh mn'yeh oh•dehb•rahch' z…*
I'm going to…	**Proszę…** *proh•sheh…*
this address	**pod ten adres** *poht tehn ahd•rehs*
the airport	**na lotnisko** *nah loht•n'ees•koh*
the train station	**na dworzec kolejowy** *nah dvoh•zhehts koh•leh•yoh•vyh*
How much?	**Ile płacę?** *ee•leh pwah•tseh*

YOU MAY HEAR…

Dokąd jedziemy? *doh•kohnt yeh•dj'yeh•myh*	Where to?
Jaki adres? *yah•kee ahd•rehs*	What's the address?

Schedule a taxi pick up by calling a local company; check the phone book for listings. You may be able to hail a taxi but make sure it displays a recognized taxi company name and that the meter is started. A table of fares should be displayed in the taxi. Fares are higher on Sundays, public holidays and at night. Be careful about taking a taxi to suburbs of the city, as it may mean entering another fare zone. Most taxis take cash only. It is not customary to tip the taxi drivers.

I'm late.	**Jestem spóźniony** *m* **/spóźniona** *f. yehs*·tehm *spoozh'·n'yoh·nyh/spoozh'·n'yoh·nah*
Can you drive faster/ slower?	**Mógłby pan jechać szybciej/wolniej?** *moogw·byh pahn yeh·hahch' shyhp·ch'yehy/vohl·n'yey*
Stop/Wait here, please.	**Proszę się tu zatrzymać/tu zaczekać.** *proh·sheh sh'yeh too zaht·shyh·mahch'/too zah·cheh·kahch'*
You said it would cost...	**Mówił pan, że to będzie kosztowało...** *moo·veew pahn zheh toh behn'·dj'yeh kohsh·toh·vah·woh...*
Keep the change.	**Proszę zatrzymać resztę.** *proh·sheh zah·tshyh·mahch' rehsh·teh*

Bicycle & Motorbike

I'd like to rent...	**Chciałbym** *m* **/Chciałabym** *f* **wynająć...** *hch'yahw·byhm/hch'yah·wah·byhm vyh·nah·yohn'ch'...*
a bicycle	**rower** *roh·vehr*
a moped	**motorower** *moh·toh·roh·vehr*
a motorcycle	**motor** *moh·tohr*
How much per day/ week?	**Ile kosztuje wynajęcie na dzień/tydzień?** *ee·leh kohsh·too·yeh vyh·nah·yehn'·ch'yeh nah dj'yehn'/ tyh·dj'yehn'*

YOU MAY HEAR...

Poproszę prawo jazdy. poh·_proh_·sheh
prah·voh _yah_·zdyh

Your driver's license, please.

Poproszę paszport. poh·_proh_·sheh _pahsh_·pohrt Your passport, please.

Proszę tutaj podpisać. _proh_·sheh _too_·tahy
poht·_pee_·sahch'

Please sign here.

Can I have a helmet/lock?	**Mogę prosić kask/blokadę?** _moh_·geh _proh_·sh'eech' kahsk/bloh·_kah_·deh

Car Hire

Where can I rent a car?	**Gdzie mogę wynająć samochód?** gdj'yeh _moh_·geh vyh·_nah_·yohn'ch' sah·_moh_·hoot
I'd like to rent...	**Chcę wynająć...** htseh vyh·_nah_·yohn'ch'...
an automatic/ a manual	**samochód z automatyczną/ręczną skrzynią biegów** sah·_moh_·hoot z ahw·toh·mah·_tyhch_·nohm/ _rehnch_·nohm skshyh·n'yohm _byeh_·goof
a car with air conditioning	**samochód z klimatyzacją** sah·_moh_·hoot sklee·mah·tyh·_zahts_·yohm
a car seat	**fotelik dziecięcy** foh·_teh_·leek dj'yeh·_ch'yehn_·tsyh
How much...?	**Ile to kosztuje...?** _ee_·leh toh kohsh·_too_·yeh...
per day/week	**za dzień/tydzień** zah dj'yehn'/_tyh_·dj'yehn'
per kilometer	**za kilometr** zah kee·_loh_·mehtr

YOU MAY SEE...

Pb 95	regular
Pb 98	premium [super]
ON	diesel
LPG	autogas

for unlimited mileage	**bez limitu kilometrów** *behs lee•mee•too kee•loh•meht•roof*
with insurance	**z ubezpieczeniem** *zoo•behs•pyeh•cheh•n'yehm*
Are there any discounts?	**Czy są jakieś zniżki?** *chyh sohm yah•kyehsh' zn'eezh•kee*

Fuel Station

Where's the next gas [petrol] station?	**Gdzie jest najbliższa stacja benzynowa?** *gdj'yeh yehst nahy•bleesh•shah stah•tsyah behn•zyh•noh•vah*
Fill it up, please.	**Do pełna, proszę.** *doh pehw•nah proh•sheh*
. . . liters, please.	**. . . litrów, proszę.** *. . . leet•roof proh•sheh*
I'll pay in cash/ by credit card.	**Zapłacę gotówką/kartą kredytową.** *zap•wah•tseh goh•toof•kohm/kahr•tohm kreh•dyh•toh•vohm*

For Numbers, see page 171.

YOU MAY HEAR...

Proszę jechać. . . *proh•sheh yeh•hahch'. . .*	You should go. . .
prosto *prohs•toh*	straight
w lewo *vleh•voh*	left
w prawo *fprah•voh*	right
na północ/południe *nah poow•nohts/ poh•wood•n'yeh*	north/south
na wschód/zachód *na fs•hoot/zah•hoot*	east/west
To jest. . . *toh yehst. . .*	It's. . .
na rogu/za rogiem *nah roh•goo/ zah roh•gyehm*	on/around the corner
naprzeciwko. . . *nah psheh•ch'eef•koh. . .*	opposite. . .
za. . . *zah. . .*	behind. . .
przy. . . *pshyh. . .*	next to. . .

YOU MAY SEE...

 DROGA JEDNOKIERUNKOWA one way

 DROGA Z PIERWSZEŃSTWEM right of way

 PRZEJŚCIE DLA PIESZYCH pedestrian crossing

 STOP stop

 ZAKAZ PARKOWANIA no parking

 ZAKAZ WJAZDU no entry

 ZAKAZ WYPRZEDZANIA passing prohibited

 ZAKAZ ZAWRACANIA no U-turn

Asking Directions

Is this the right road to...?	**Czy to właściwa droga do...?** *chyh toh vwahsh'·ch'ee·vah droh·gah doh...*
How far is it to...?	**Jak daleko jest stąd do...?** *yahk dah·leh·koh yehst stohnt doh...*
Where's...?	**Gdzie jest...?** *gdj'yeh yehst...*
...Street	**ulica...** *oo·lee·tsah...*
this address	**ten adres** *tehn ahd·rehs*
the highway [motorway]	**autostrada** *ahw·toh·strah·dah*

| Can you show me on the map? | **Czy może mi pan pokazać na mapie?** *chyh moh·zheh mee pahn poh·kah·zahch' nah mah·pyeh* |
| I'm lost. | **Zgubiłem m /Zgubiłam f się.** *zgoo·bee·wehm/ zgoo·bee·wahm sh'yeh* |

Parking

Can I park here?	**Czy mogę tu zaparkować?** *chyh moh·geh too zah·pahr·koh·vahch'*
Where is the nearest parking lot [car park]?	**Gdzie jest najbliższy parking?** *gdj'yeh yehst nahy·bleesh·shyh pahr·keenk*
How much…?	**Ile kosztuje…?** *ee·leh kohsh·too·yeh…*
per hour	**godzina** *goh·dj'ee·nah*
per day	**dzień** *dj'yehn'*
for overnight	**zostawienie samochodu na noc** *zohs·tah·vyeh·n'yeh sah·moh·hoh·doo nah nohts*

Breakdown & Repair

My car broke down/ won't start.	**Mój samochód się zepsuł/nie chce zapalić.** *mooy sah·moh·hoot sh'yeh zehp·soow/n'yeh htseh zah·pah·leech'*
Can you fix it (today)?	**Możecie to naprawić (dzisiaj)?** *moh·zheh·ch'yeh toh nahp·rah·veech' (dj'ee·sh'yahy)*
When can I pick up the car?	**Kiedy mogę odebrać samochód?** *kyeh·dyh moh·geh oh·dehb·rahch' sah·moh·hoot*
How much?	**Ile to kosztuje?** *ee·leh toh kohsh·too·yeh*

Accidents

| There was an accident. | **Był wypadek.** *byhw vyh·pah·dehk* |
| Call an ambulance/ the police. | **Proszę wezwać karetkę/policję.** *proh·sheh vehz·vahch' kah·reht·keh/poh·leets·yeh* |

Places to Stay

ESSENTIAL

Can you recommend a hotel?	**Czy może mi pan polecić jakiś hotel?** _chyh moh·zheh mee pahn poh·leh·ch'eech' yah·keesh' hoh·tehl_
I have a reservation.	**Mam rezerwację.** _mahm reh·zehr·vahts·yeh_
My name is...	**Nazywam się...** _nah·zyh·vahm sh'yeh..._
I would like a room...	**Chciałbym** _m_ /**Chciałabym** _f_ **wynająć pokój...** _hch'yahw·byhm/hch'yah·wah·byhm vyh·nah·yohn'ch' poh·kooy..._
for one/two	**jednoosobowy/dwuosobowy** _yehd·noh·oh·soh·boh·vyh/dvoo·oh·soh·boh·vyh_
with a bathroom	**z łazienką** _zwah·zh'yehn·kohm_
with air conditioning	**z klimatyzacją** _sklee·mah·tyh·zahts·yohm_
For...	**Na...** _nah..._
tonight	**tę noc** _teh nohts_
two nights	**dwie noce** _dvyeh noh·tseh_
one week	**tydzień** _tyh·dj'yehn'_
How much?	**Ile to kosztuje?** _ee·leh toh kohsh·too·yeh_
Do you have anything cheaper?	**Czy są jakieś tańsze pokoje?** _chyh sohm yah·kyehsh' tahn'·sheh poh·koh·yeh_
When's check-out?	**O której mamy zwolnić pokój?** _oh ktoo·rehy mah·myh zvohl·n'eech' poh·kooy_
Can I leave this in the safe?	**Mogę zostawić to w sejfie?** _moh·geh zohs·tah·veech' toh fsehy·fyeh_
Can I leave my luggage?	**Mogę zostawić mój bagaż?** _moh·geh zohs·tah·veech' mooy bah·gahsh_

| Can I have the bill/ a receipt? | **Czy mogę prosić o rachunek/pokwitowanie?** *chyh moh·geh pro·sh'eech' oh rah·hoo·nehk/ poh·kfee·toh·vah·n'yeh* |
| I'll pay in cash/ by credit card. | **Zapłacę gotówką/kartą kredytową.** *zah·pwah·tseh goh·toof·kohm/kahr·tohm kreh·dyh·toh·vohm* |

Somewhere to Stay

Can you recommend a hotel?	**Czy może mi pan polecić jakiś hotel?** *chyh moh·zheh mee pahn poh·leh·ch'eech' yah·keesh' hoh·tehl*
What is it near?	**Koło czego on się znajduje?** *koh·woh cheh·goh ohn sh'yeh znahy·doo·yeh*
How do I get there?	**Jak można się tam dostać?** *yahk mohzh·nah sh'yeh tahm dohs·tahch'*

At the Hotel

I have a reservation.	**Mam rezerwację.** *mahm reh·zehr·vahts·yeh*
My name is...	**Nazywam się...** *nah·zyh·vahm sh'yeh...*
I would like a room...	**Chciałbym** *m* /**Chciałabym** *f* **wynająć pokój...** *hch'yahw·byhm/hch'yah·wah·byhm vyh·nah·yohnch' poh·kooy...*
with a bathroom	**z łazienką** *zwah·zh'yehn·kohm*
with air conditioning	**z klimatyzacją** *sklee·mah·tyh·zahts·yohm*

If you have nowhere to stay booked on arrival, visit the local **Informacja Turystyczna** (Tourist Information Office) for recommendations on places to stay. These are usually located in the city center and/or near the train station.

There is a wide choice of places to stay; prices vary according to facilities, location and season. Following are some places to stay.

Hotels: As any other country, Poland has numerous hotels catering to leisure and business travelers. In smaller towns you will mainly find lower class hotels.

Hostels: These are inexpensive, and usually offer both private and dormitory-style rooms.

Tourist Houses: **Domy Turysty** (guest houses), ideal for budget travelers, are run by the **PTTK** (Polish Tourist Country Lovers' Society), which also runs **schroniska górskie** (mountain hostels). These are found mainly in the countryside.

There are many **pensjonaty** (boarding houses) and **pokoje gościnne** (rooms in private houses) available in big towns and resorts, some of which can be found on the internet. In some towns you may book a room through certain tourist agencies, such as **Biuro Kwater Prywatnych** or **Agencja Promocji Miasta**. Most pensjonaty provide meals and/or cooking facilities. They can accommodate fewer guests than hotels but offer a friendly and cozy atmosphere.

for smokers/ non-smokers	**dla palących/niepalących**	*dla pah·lohn·tsyhh/ n'yeh·pah·lohn·tsyhh*
For...	**Na...**	*nah...*
tonight	**tę noc**	*teh nohts*
two nights	**dwie noce**	*dvyeh noh·tseh*
one week	**tydzień**	*tyh·dj'yehn'*
Does the hotel have...?	**Czy jest u państwa...?**	*chyh yehst oo pahn's·tfah...*
a computer for guests	**komputer dla gości**	*kohm·poo·tehr dlah gohsh'·ch'ee*

an elevator [a lift]	**winda** _veen·dah_	
(wireless) internet service	**(bezprzewodowy) internet** _(behs·psheh·voh·doh·vyh) een·tehr·neht_	
room service	**room service** _room sehr·vees_	
a pool	**basen** _bah·sehn_	
a gym	**siłownia** _sh'ee·wohv·n'yah_	
Could I have...?	**Czy mógłbym _m_/mogłabym _f_ dostać...?** _chyh moogw·byhm/moh·gwah·byhm dohs·tahch'..._	
an extra bed	**dodatkowe łóżko** _doh·daht·koh·veh woozh·koh_	

YOU MAY HEAR...

Poproszę pana paszport/kartę kredytową. _poh·proh·sheh pah·nah pahsh·pohrt/kahr·teh kreh·dyh·toh·vohm_ — Your passport/credit card, please.

Proszę wypełnić ten formularz. _proh·sheh vyh·pehw·n'eech' tehn fohr·moo·lahsh_ — Please fill out this form.

Proszę tutaj podpisać. _proh·sheh too·tahy poht·pee·sahch'_ — Please sign here.

| a cot | **rozkładane łóżko** *rohs-kwah-dah-neh woozh-koh* |
| a crib [child's cot] | **łóżeczko dziecięce** *woo-zhehch-koh dj'yeh-ch'yehn-tseh* |

For Numbers, see page 171.

Price

| How much per night/ week? | **Jaka jest cena za noc/tydzień?** *yah-kah yehst tseh-nah zah nohts/tyh-dj'yehn'* |
| Does the price include breakfast/sales tax [VAT]? | **Czy w cenę wliczone jest śniadanie/wliczony jest VAT?** *chyh f tseh-neh vlee-choh-neh yehst sh'n'yah-dah-n'yeh/vlee-choh-nyh yehst vaht* |

Preferences

Can I see the room?	**Czy mógłbym m /mogłabym f zobaczyć ten pokój?** *chyh moogw-byhm/moh-gwah-byhm zoh-bah-chyhch' tehn poh-kooy*
I'd like a...room.	**Chciałbym m /Chciałabym f ... pokój.** *hch'yahw-byhm/hch'yah-wah-byhm ... poh-kooy*
better	**lepszy** *lehp-shyh*
bigger	**większy** *vyehn-kshyh*
cheaper	**tańszy** *tahn'-shyh*
quieter	**cichszy** *ch'ee-hshyh*
I'll take it.	**Wezmę ten pokój** *vehz-meh tehn poh-kooy*
No, I won't take it.	**Nie, nie chcę tego pokoju** *n'yeh, n'yeh htseh teh-goh poh-koh-yoo*

Questions

Where is/are...?	**Gdzie jest/są...?** *gdj'eh yehst/sohm...*
the bar	**bar** *bahr*
the bathrooms [toilets]	**toaleta** *toh-ah-leh-tah*
the elevators [lifts]	**windy** *veen-dyh*

Can I have…?	**Czy mogę dostać…?** *chyh moh•geh dohs•tahch'…*
a blanket	**koc** *kohts*
an iron	**żelazko** *zheh•lahs•koh*
a pillow	**poduszkę** *poh•doosh•keh*
soap	**mydło** *myhd•woh*
toilet paper	**papier toaletowy** *pah•pyehr toh•ah•leh•toh•vyh*
a towel	**ręcznik** *rehnch•n'eek*
Do you have an adapter for this?	**Czy ma pan do tego przejściówkę?** *chyh mah pahn doh teh•goh pshehysh'•ch'yoof•keh*
How do I turn on the lights?	**Jak się włącza światło?** *yahk sh'yeh vwohn•chah sh'fyaht•woh*
Please wake me at…	**Proszę mnie obudzić o…** *proh•sheh mn'yeh oh•boo•dj'eech' oh…*
Could I have my things from the safe?	**Mógłbym** *m* **/Mogłabym** *f* **wyjąć moje rzeczy z sejfu?** *moogw•byhm/moh•gwah•byhm vyh•yohn'ch' moh•yeh zheh•chyh ssehy•foo*
Can I leave this in the safe?	**Czy mogę to zostawić w sejfie?** *chyh moh•geh toh zohs•tah•veech' fsehy•fyeh*
Is there any mail [post] for me?	**Czy są jakieś listy do mnie?** *chyh sohm yah•kyehsh' lees•tyh doh mn'yeh*

YOU MAY SEE...

PCHAĆ/CIĄGNĄĆ	push/pull
TOALETA	bathrooms [toilet]
PRYSZNICE	showers
WINDY	elevators [lifts]
SCHODY	stairs
PRALNIA	laundry
NIE PRZESZKADZAĆ	do not disturb
DRZWI PRZECIWPOŻAROWE	fire door
WYJŚCIE (AWARYJNE)	(emergency) exit
BUDZENIE TELEFONICZNE	wake-up call

Are there any messages for me? **Czy są dla mnie jakieś wiadomości?** *chyh sohm dlah mn'yeh yah-kyehsh' vyah-doh-mosh'-ch'ee*

Do you have a laundry service? **Czy świadczycie Państwo usługę prania odzieży?** *chyh sh'vyaht-chyh-ch'yeh pahn'-stvoh oo-swoo-geh prah-n'yah oh-dj'yeh-zhy*

Problems

There's a problem. **Mam problem.** *mahm prohb-lehm*

I've lost my key. **Zgubiłem m /Zgubiłam f klucz.** *zgoo-bee-wehm/ zgoo-bee-wahm klooch*

I've locked the key in my room. **Zatrzasnąłem m /Zatrzasnęłam f klucz w pokoju.** *zah-tshahs-noh-wehm/zah-tshahs-neh-wahm klooch fpoh-koh-yoo*

Poland's electricity is 230 volts. You may need a converter and/ or an adapter for your appliance.

The room is dirty.	**Pokój jest brudny.**	*poh•kooy yehst brood•nyh*
There are bugs in my room.	**W moim pokoju są robaki.**	*vmoh•eem poh•koh•yoo sohm roh•bah•kee*
There is no hot water/ toilet paper.	**Nie ma ciepłej wody/papieru toaletowego.**	*n'yeh mah ch'yehp•wehy voh•dyh/pah•pyeh•roo toh•ah•leh•toh•veh•goh*
...doesn't work.	**...nie działa.**	*...n'yeh dj'yah•wah*
Can you fix...?	**Mogą państwo naprawić...?**	*moh•gohm pahn's•tfoh nahp•rah•veech'...*
the air conditioning	**klimatyzację**	*klee•mah•tyh•zahts•yeh*
the fan	**wentylator**	*vehn•tyh•lah•tohr*
he heat [heating]	**ogrzewanie**	*oh•gzheh•vah•n'yeh*
the light	**światło**	*sh'fyaht•woh*
the TV	**telewizor**	*teh•leh•vee•zohr*
the toilet	**toaletę**	*toh•ah•leh•teh*
I'd like another room.	**Chciałbym** *m* **/Chciałabym** *f* **zmienić pokój.**	*hch'yahw•byh /hch'yah•wah•byhm zmyeh•n'eech' poh•kooy*

Checking Out

When's check-out?	**O której mam zwolnić pokój?**	*oh ktoo•rehy mahm zvohl•n'eech' poh•kooy*
Could I leave my bags here until...?	**Czy mogę zostawić tutaj bagaż do...?**	*chyh moh•geh zohs•tah•veech' too•tahy bah•gahsh doh...*
Can I have an itemized bill/a receipt?	**Czy mogę dostać szczegółowy rachunek/ pokwitowanie?**	*chyh moh•geh dohs•tach' shcheh•goo•woh•vyh ra•hoo•nehk/poh•kfee•toh•vah•n'yeh*
I think there's a mistake in this bill.	**Na tym rachunku chyba jest błąd.**	*nah tyhm rah•hoon•koo hyh•bah yehst blohnt*
I'll pay in cash/by credit card.	**Zapłacę gotówką/kartą kredytową.**	*zah•pwah•tseh goh•toof•kohm/kahr•tohm kreh•dyh•toh•vohm*

Renting

I've reserved an apartment/a room.	**Zarezerwowałem** *m* **/Zarezerwowałam** *f* **mieszkanie/pokój.** *zah·reh·zehr·voh·vah·wehm/ zah·reh·zehr·voh·vah·lahm myehsh·kah·n'yeh/poh·kooy*
My name is...	**Nazywam się...** *nah·zyh·vahm sh'yeh...*
Can I have the key/ key card?	**Czy mogę dostać klucz/kartę?** *chyh moh·geh dohs·tahch' klooch/kahr·teh*
Are there...?	**Czy są...?** *chyh sohm...*
dishes [crockery]	**naczynia** *nah·chyh·n'yah*
pillows	**poduszki** *poh·doosh·kee*
Are there...?	**Czy są/jest...?** *chyh sohm/yehst...*
sheets	**pościel** *pohsh'·ch'yehl*
towels	**ręczniki** *rehnch·n'ee·kee*
kitchen utensils	**sztućce** *shtooch'·tseh*

When do I put out the bins?	**Kiedy wywożą śmieci?** _kyeh·dyh vyh·voh·zhohm sh'myeh·ch'ee_
...is broken.	**...nie działa.** ..._n'yeh dj'yah·wah_
How does...work?	**Jak obsługiwać...?** _yahk ohp·swoo·gee·vahch'..._
the air conditioner	**klimatyzator** _klee·mah·tyh·zah·tohr_
the dishwasher	**zmywarkę** _zmyh·vahr·keh_
the freezer	**zamrażarkę** _zahm·rah·zhahr·keh_
the heater	**grzejnik** _gzhehy·n'eek_
the microwave	**mikrofalówkę** _mee·kroh·fah·loof·keh_
the refrigerator	**lodówkę** _loh·doof·keh_
the stove	**kuchenkę** _koo·hehn·keh_
the washing machine	**pralkę** _prahl·keh_

Domestic Items

Could I have...?	**Czy mogę dostać...?** _chyh moh·geh dohs·tahch'..._
an adapter	**przejściówkę** _pshehysh'·ch'yoof·keh_
aluminum [kitchen] foil	**folię aluminiową** _fohl·yeh ah·loo·mee·n'yoh·vohm_
a bottle opener	**otwieracz do butelek** _oht·fyeh·rahch doh boo·teh·lehk_
a broom	**zmiotkę** _zmyoht·keh_
a can opener	**otwieracz do puszek** _oht·fyeh·rahch doh poo·shehk_
a corkscrew	**korkociąg** _kohr·koh·ch'yohnk_
bin bags	**worki na śmieci** _vohr·kee nah sh'myeh·ch'ee_
matches	**zapałki** _zah·pahw·kee_
a mop	**mopa** _moh·pah_
napkins	**serwetki** _sehr·veht·kee_
paper towels	**papierowe ręczniki** _pah·pyeh·roh·veh rehnch·n'ee·kee_
plastic wrap [cling film]	**folię do żywności** _fohl·yeh doh zhyhv·nohsh'·ch'ee_

a plunger	**przepychacz** *psheh•pyh•hahch*
scissors	**nożyczki** *noh•zhyhch•kee*
a vacuum cleaner	**odkurzacz** *oht•koo•zhahch*

At the Hostel

Do you have any places left for tonight?	**Czy są na dzisiaj wolne miejsca?** *chyh sohm nah dj'ee•sh'yahy vohl•neh myehys•tsah*
I would like a single/ double room.	**Chciałbym** m /**Chciałabym** f **pokój jednoosobowy/ dwuosobowy.** *hch'yahw•byhm/hch'yah•wah•byhm poh•kooy yehd•noh•oh•soh•boh•vyh/dvoo•oh•soh•boh•vyh*
Could I have…?	**Czy mógłbym** m /**mogłabym** f **dostać…?** *chyh moogw•byhm/moh•gwah•byhm dohs•tahch'…*
a blanket	**koc** *kohts*
a pillow	**poduszkę** *poh•doosh•keh*
sheets	**pościel** *pohsh'•ch'yehl*
a towel	**ręcznik** *rehnch•n'eek*
Do you have lockers?	**Czy są tu zamykane schowki?** *Chyh sohm too zah•myh•kah•neh s•hohv•kee*
When do you lock up?	**O której zamykają państwo drzwi?** *oh ktoo•rehy zah•myh•kah•yohm pahn'•stfoh djvee*
Do I need a membership card?	**Czy potrzebuję karty członkowskiej** *Chyh poh•tsheh•boo•yeh kahr•tyh chwohn•kohv•skyehy*
Here's my international student card.	**Oto moja międzynarodowa karta studencka** *oh•toh moh•yah myehn•dzyh•nah•roh•doh•vah kahr•tah stoo•dehn•tskah*

Going Camping

| Can I camp here? | **Mogę tutaj rozbić namiot?** *moh•geh too•tahy rohz•beech' nah•myoht* |
| Is there a campsite near here? | **Czy jest tu w pobliżu jakiś camping?** *chyh yehst too fpoh•blee•zhoo yah•keesh' kehm•peenk* |

What is the charge per day/week?	**Ile kosztuje jedna noc/tydzień?** _ee·leh_ _kohsh·too·yeh yehd·nah nohts/tyh·dj'yehn'_
Are there …?	**Czy są/jest** _chyh sohm/yehst_
electric outlets	**gniazdka elektryczne** _gn'yahs·tkah eh·lehk·tryh·chneh_
showers?	**prysznice?** _pryhsh·n'ee·tseh_
laundry facilities	**pralnia** _prahl·n'yah_
tents for hire	**namioty do wynajęcia** _nah·myoh·tyh doh_ _vyh·nah·yehn·ch'yah_
Where can I empty the chemical toilet?	**Gdzie mogę opróżnić chemiczną toaletę?** _gd'yeh moh·geh ohp·roozh·n'eech'_ _heh·meech·nohm toh·ah·leh·teh_

For Domestic Items, see page 45.

For In the Kitchen, see page 75.

47

Communications

ESSENTIAL

Is there an internet cafe nearby?	**Czy jest tu gdzieś w pobliżu kafejka internetowa?** _chyh yehst too gj'yehsh' fpoh·blee·zhoo_ _kah·fehy·kah een·tehr·neh·toh·vah_
Can I access the internet/check e-mails?	**Można tu skorzystać z internetu/sprawdzić pocztę?** _mohzh·nah too skoh·zhyhs·tahch'_ _zeen·tehr·neh·too/sprahw·dj'eech' pohch·teh_
How much per hour/ half hour?	**Ile kosztuje godzina/pół godziny?** _ee·leh_ _koh·shtoo·yeh goh·dj'ee·nah/poow goh·dj'ee·nyh_
How do I connect/ log on?	**Jak mam się połączyć z siecią/zalogować?** _yahk_ _mahm sh'yeh poh·wohn·chyhch' ssh'yeh·ch'yohm/_ _zah·loh·goh·vahch'_

Is there a password?	**Jest jakieś hasło?** *yehst yah·kyehsh' hahs·woh*
A phone card, please.	**Poproszę kartę telefoniczną.** *poh·proh·sheh kahr·teh teh·leh·foh·n'eech·nohm*
Can I have your phone number?	**Czy mogę prosić pana numer telefonu?** *chyh moh·geh proh·sh'eech' pah·nah noo·mehr teh·leh·foh·noo*
Here's my number/ e-mail address.	**To jest mój numer telefonu/adres e-mail.** *toh yehst mooy noo·mehr teh·leh·foh·noo/ ahd·rehs ee·mehyl*
Can you call me please/e-mail me?	**Czy mógłby pan do mnie zadzwonić/napisać do mnie maila?** *chyh moogw·byh pahn doh mn'yeh zahdz·voh·n'eech'/nah·pee·sahch' doh mn'yeh mehy·lah*
Hello. This is...	**Dzień dobry. Mówi...** *dj'yehn' dohb·ryh moo·vee...*
I'd like to speak to...	**Chciałbym** *m* **/Chciałabym** *f* **rozmawiać z...** *hch'yahw·byhm/hch'yah·wah·byhm rohz·mah·vyahch' z...*
Could you repeat that?	**Może pan powtórzyć?** *moh·zheh pahn pohf·too·zhyhch'*
I'll call back later.	**Zadzwonię później.** *zahdz·voh·n'yeh poozh'·n'yehy*
Bye.	**Do widzenia.** *doh vee·dzeh·n'yah*
Where's the post office?	**Gdzie jest poczta?** *Gdj'yeh yehst pohch·tah*
I'd like to send this to...	**Chciałbym** *m* **/Chciałabym** *f* **to wysłać do...** *hch'yahw·byhm/hch'yah·wah·byhm toh vyhs·wahch' doh...*

Online

Is there an internet cafe nearby?	**Czy jest tu gdzieś w pobliżu kafejka internetowa?** *chyh yehst too gdj'yehsh' fpoh·blee·zhoo kah·fehy·kah een·tehr·neh·toh·vah*
Does it have wireless internet?	**Jest tam bezprzewodowy internet?** *yehst tahm behs·psheh·voh·doh·vyh een·tehr·neht*
What is the WiFi password?	**Jakie jest hasło do sieci WiFi?** *yah·kyeh yehst hahs·woh doh sh'yeh·ch'ee vee phee*
Is the WiFi free?	**Czy korzystanie z WiFi jest bezpłatne?** *chyh koh·zhyh·stah·nyeh z vee phee yehst behs·pwaht·neh*
Do you have bluetooth?	**masz funkcję Bluetooth?** *mahsh foon·ktsyeh bloo·tooth*
How do I turn the computer on/off?	**Jak włączyć/wyłączyć komputer?** *yak vwohn·chych'/wyh·wohn·chych' kohm·poo·tehr*
How much per hour/ half hour?	**Ile kosztuje godzina/pół godziny?** *ee·leh kohsh·too·yeh goh·dj'ee·nah/poow goh·dj'ee·nyh*
Can I...?	**Mogę...?** *moh·geh...*
access the internet	**skorzystać z internetu** *skoh·zhyhs·tahch' zeen·tehr·neh·too*
check e-mail	**sprawdzić pocztę** *sprahv·dj'eech' pohch·teh*

print something	**coś wydrukować** *tsohsh' vyh·droo·<u>koh</u>·vahch'*
access Skype?	**używać Skype'a?** *ooh·<u>zhyh</u>·vahch' <u>skahy</u>·pah*
plug in/charge my laptop/iPhone/ iPad/BlackBerry?	**podłączyć/naładować laptopa/iPhone'a/ iPada/Blackberry?** *pohd·<u>wohn</u>·chyhch'/ nah·wah·<u>doh</u>·vach' lahp·<u>toh</u>·pah/ahy·<u>foh</u>·nah/ ahy·<u>pah</u>·dah/blahk·<u>beh</u>·ryh*
How do I...? connect/ disconnect	**Jak mam się...?** *yahk mahm sh'yeh...* **połączyć z siecią/rozłączyć** *poh·<u>wohn</u>·chyhch' <u>ssh'yeh</u>·ch'yohm/rohz·<u>wohn</u>·chyhch'*
log on/off	**zalogować/wylogować** *zah·loh·<u>goh</u>·vahch'/ wyh·loh·<u>goh</u>·vahch'*
How do I type this symbol?	**Jak wpisać ten symbol?** *yahk <u>fpee</u>·sahch' tehn <u>syhm</u>·bohl*

YOU MAY SEE...

ZAMKNIJ	close
USUŃ	delete
E-MAIL	e-mail
ZAKOŃCZ	exit
POMOC	help
KOMUNIKATOR	instant messenger
ZALOGUJ SIĘ	login
ANULUJ	cancel
OTWARTE	open
DRUKUJ	print
ZAPISZ	save
NAZWA UŻYTKOWNIKA	username
HASŁO	password
(BEZPRZEWODOWY) INTERNET	(wireless) internet

What's your e-mail?	**Jaki jest pana adres e-mail?** _yah_•kee yehst _pah_•nah _ahd_•rehs _ee_•mehyl
My e-mail is...	**Mój e-mail to...** mooy _ee_•meyhl toh...
Do you have a scanner?	**Czy jest tu skaner?** Chyh yehst too _skah_•nehr

Social Media

Are you on Facebook/ Twitter?	**Masz konto na Facebooku/Twitterze?** mahsh _kohn_•toh nah fehys•_boo_•koo/twee•_teh_•zheh
What's your user name?	**Pod jaką nazwą masz konto?** pohd _yah_•kohm _nahz_•vohm mahsh _kohn_•toh
I'll add you as a friend.	**Dodam Cię do znajomych.** _doh_•dahm ch'yeh doh znah•_yoh_•myhh
I'll follow you on Twitter.	**Będę śledził/śledziła twoje wpisy na Twitterze.** _behn_•deh sh'leh•'dj'eewh/sh'leh•'_dj'ee_•wah tfoh•yeh fpee•syh nah twee•_teh_•zheh
Are you following...?	**Czy śledzisz wpisy....?** chyh _sh'leh_•dj'eesh _fpee_•syh...
I'll put the pictures on Facebook/Twitter.	**Wrzucę zdjęcia na Facebooka/Twittera.** _vzhoo_•tseh _zdyehn_•chy'ahh nah fehys•_boo_•kah/ twee•_teh_•rah
I'll tag you in the pictures.	**Zaznaczę cię na zdjęciach.** zah•_znah_•cheh ch'yeh nah _zdyehn_•chy'ahh

Phone

A phone card, please.	**Poproszę kartę telefoniczną.** poh•_proh_•sheh _kahr_•teh teh•leh•foh•_n'eech_•nohm
How much?	**Ile to kosztuje?** _ee_•leh toh kohsh•_too_•yeh
My phone doesn't work here.	**Mój telefon tu nie działa.** mooy teh•_leh_•fohn too n'yeh _dj'yah_•wah
What's the country code for...?	**Jaki jest numer kierunkowy do...?** _yah_•kee yehst _noo_•mehr kyeh•roon•_koh_•vyh doh...

Public phones are card operated. A local or international **karta telefoniczna** (phone card) can be purchased from kiosks or post offices. Be sure to break off the perforated corner before inserting the card into the phone.

What's the number for Information?	**Jaki jest numer do informacji?** *yah·kee yehst noo·mehr doh een·fohr·mahts·yee*
I'd like the number for…	**Proszę o numer telefonu do…** *proh·sh'eh oh noo·mehr teh·leh·foh·noo doh…*
My phone doesn't work here.	**Mój telefon tu nie działa.** *mooy teh·leh·fohn too n'yeh dj'yah·wah*
What network are you on?	**W jakiej jesteś sieci?** *vyah·kyey yehs·tehsh' sh'yeh·ch'ee*
Is it 3G?	**Czy jest to sieć 3G?** *tchyh yehst toh shy'ech' tshyh gyeh*
I have run out of credit/minutes.	**Skończyła mi się karta.** *skohn'·chyh·wah mee sh'yeh kahr·tah*
Can I buy some credit?	**Czy mogę tu doładować kartę?** *tchyh moh·geh tooh doh·wah·doh·vahch' kahr·teh*
Do you have a phone charger?	**Czy ma Pan m / Pani f ładowarkę do telefonu?** *chyh mah pahn/ pahnee wah·doh·vahr·keh doh teh·leh·foh·noo*
Can I have your phone number?	**Czy mogę dostać twój numer telefonu?** *chyh moh·geh doh·stahch' tfooy noo·mehr teh·leh·foh·noo*
Here's my number.	**Oto mój numer telefonu.** *oh·toh mooy noo·mehr teh·leh·foh·noo*
Please call/text me.	**Zadzwoń do mnie/przyślij mi SMS.** *zah·dzvohn' doh mnyeh/pshyh·sh'leey mee ehs·ehm·ehs*

| I'll call/text you. | **Zadzwonię do ciebie/wyślę ci SMS.** *zah·dzvoh·n'yeh* |
| | *doh ch'yeh·byeh/vyh·sh'leh ch'ee ehs·ehm·ehs* |

For Numbers, see page 171.

Telephone Etiquette

Hello. This is...	**Dzień dobry. Mówi...** *dj'yen' dohb·ryh moo·vee...*
I'd like to speak to...	**Chciałbym** *m* / **Chciałabym** *f* **rozmawiać z...**
	hch'yahw·byhm/hch'yah·wah·byhm
	rohz·mah·vyahch' z...
Extension...	**Wewnętrzny...** *vehv·nehntsh·nyh...*
Speak louder/more	**Proszę mówić głośniej/wolniej.** *proh·sh'eh*
slowly, please.	*moo·veech' gwohsh'·n'yehy/vohl·n'yehy*

YOU MAY HEAR...

Halo. *hah·loh*	Hello.
Przepraszam, kto mówi? *psheh·prah·shahm*	Who's calling, please?
ktoh moo·vee	
Proszę poczekać. *proh·sheh poh·cheh·kahch'*	Please hold.
Przełączę pana. *psheh·wohn·cheh pah·nah*	I'll put you through.
Nie może teraz podejść. *n'yeh moh·zheh*	He/She can't come to
teh·rahs poh·deysh'ch'	the phone.
Coś przekazać? *tsohsh' psheh·kah·zahch'*	Would you like to leave
	a message?
Czy może do pana oddzwonić? *chyh*	Can he/she call you back?
moh·zheh doh pah·nah ohd·dzvoh·n'eech'	
Jaki jest pana numer telefonu? *yah·kee*	What's your number?
yehst pah·nah noo·mehr teh·leh·foh·noo	

Could you repeat that?	**Mógłby pan powtórzyć?** _moogw•byh pahn pohf•too•zhyhch'_
I'll call back later.	**Zadzwonię później.** _zahdz•voh•n'yeh poozh'•n'yehy_
Bye.	**Do widzenia.** _doh vee•dzeh•n'yah_

Fax

Can I send/receive a fax here?	**Czy mogę stąd wysłać/tu odebrać faks?** _chyh moh•geh stohnt vyhs•wahch'/too oh•dehb•rahch' fahks_
What's the fax number?	**Jaki jest numer faksu?** _yah•kee yehst noo•mehr fahk•soo_
Please fax this to...	**Proszę to przefaksować do...** _proh•sheh toh psheh•fahk•soh•vahch' doh..._

YOU MAY HEAR...

Proszę wypełnić deklarację celną. _proh•sheh vyh•pehw•n'eech' deh•klah•rahts•yeh tsehl•nohm_ Please fill out the customs declaration form.

Jaka jest wartość przesyłki? _yah•kah yehst wahr•tohshch' psheh•syhw•kee_ What's the value of the package?

Co jest w środku? _tsoh yehst fsh'roht•koo_ What's inside?

Poczta (the post office) has locations throughout Poland. It handles mail and provides courier, phone and fax services. Stamps and postcards can be bought at the post office and at some kiosks. Mailboxes are red and display the logo **Poczta Polska**.

Post

Where's the post office/ mailbox [postbox]?	**Gdzie jest poczta/skrzynka pocztowa?** *gdj'yeh yehst pohch·tah/skshyhn·kah pohch·toh·vah*
A stamp for this postcard/letter, please.	**Poproszę znaczek na tę pocztówkę/ten list.** *poh·proh·sheh znah·chehk nah teh pohch·toof·keh/ tehn leest*
How much?	**Ile to kosztuje?** *ee·leh toh kohsh·too·yeh*
I want to send this package by airmail/ express mail.	**Chcę wysłać tę paczkę pocztą lotniczą/ priorytetem.** *htseh vyhs·wahch' teh pahch·keh pohch·tohm loht·n'ee·chohm/pryoh·ryh·teh·tehm*
A receipt, please.	**Poproszę paragon.** *poh·proh·sheh pah·rah·gohn*

Food & Drink

ESSENTIAL

Can you recommend a good restaurant/ cafe?	**Czy może mi pan polecić dobrą restaurację/ kawiarnię?** *chyh* <u>*moh*</u>*·zheh mee pahn poh·leh·ch'eech'* <u>*dohb*</u>*·rohm rehs·tahw·*<u>*rahts*</u>*·yeh/ kah·*<u>*vyahr*</u>*·n'yeh*
Is there a traditional Polish/an inexpensive restaurant nearby?	**Czy jest tu gdzieś w pobliżu tradycyjna polska/niedroga restauracja?** *chyh yehst too gdj'yehsh' fpoh·*<u>*blee*</u>*·zhoo trah·dyh·*<u>*tsyhy*</u>*·nah* <u>*pohls*</u>*·kah/n'yeh·*<u>*droh*</u>*·gah rehs·tahw·*<u>*rahts*</u>*·yah*
A table for one/two, please.	**Stolik dla jednej osoby/dwóch osób, proszę.** <u>*stoh*</u>*·leek dlah* <u>*yehd*</u>*·nehy oh·*<u>*soh*</u>*·byh/dvooh oh·*<u>*soop*</u> <u>*proh*</u>*·sheh*
Can we sit...?	**Możemy usiąść...?** *moh·*<u>*zheh*</u>*·myh* <u>*oo*</u>*·sh'yohn'sh'ch'...*
here/there	**tu/tam** *too/tahm*
outside	**na zewnątrz** *nah* <u>*zehv*</u>*·nohntsh*
in a non-smoking area	**w części dla niepalących** <u>*fchehn'sh'*</u>*·ch'ee dlah n'yeh·pah·*<u>*lohn*</u>*·tsyhh*
Where are the toilets?	**Gdzie są toalety?** *gdj'yeh sohm toh·ah·*<u>*leh*</u>*·tyh*
Can I have a menu?	**Mogę prosić menu?** <u>*moh*</u>*·geh* <u>*proh*</u>*·sh'eech' meh·*<u>*n'ee*</u>
What do you recommend?	**Co może pan polecić?** *tsoh* <u>*moh*</u>*·zheh pahn poh·*<u>*leh*</u>*·ch'eech'*
I'd like...	**Poproszę...** *poh·*<u>*proh*</u>*·sheh...*
Some more..., please.	**Poproszę trochę więcej...** *poh·*<u>*proh*</u>*·sheh troh·heh* <u>*vyehn*</u>*·tsehy...*
Enjoy your meal.	**Smacznego.** *smahch·*<u>*neh*</u>*·goh*
The check [bill], please.	**Poproszę rachunek.** *poh·*<u>*proh*</u>*·sheh rah·*<u>*hoo*</u>*·nehk*

Is service included?	**Czy obsługa jest wliczona w cenę?** *chyh ohp·swoo·gah yehst vlee·choh·nah ftseh·neh*
Can I pay by credit card?	**Czy mogę zapłacić kartą kredytową?** *chyh moh·geh zah·pwah·ch'eech' kahr·tohm kreh·dyh·toh·vohm*
Can I have a receipt?	**Czy mogę prosić paragon?** *chyh moh·geh pro·sh'eech' pah·rah·gohn*
Thank you.	**Dziękuję.** *dj'yehn·koo·yeh*

Where to Eat

Can you recommend…?	**Czy może pan polecić…?** *chyh moh·zheh pahn poh·leh·ch'eech'…*
a restaurant	**restaurację** *rehs·tahw·rahts·yeh*
a bar	**bar** *bahr*
a cafe	**kawiarnię** *kah·vyahr·n'yeh*
a fast-food place	**fast-food** *fahst·foot*
an ice-cream parlor	**lodziarnię** *loh·dj'yahr·n'yeh*
a pub	**pub** *pahp*
a cheap restaurant	**niedroga restauracja** *n'yeh·droh·gah rehs·tahw·rahts·yah*
an expensive restaurant	**droga restauracja** *droh·gah rehs·tahw·rahts·yah*
a restaurant with a good view	**restauracja z dobrym widokiem** *rehs·tahw·rahts·yah zdohb·ryhm vee·doh·kyehm*
an authentic/a non-touristy restaurant	**tradycyjna restauracja/restauracja lubiana przez miejscowych** *trah·dyh·tsyhy·nah rehs·tahw·rahts·yah / rehs·tahw·rahts·yah loo·byah·nah pshez myehys·tsoh·vyh*

Reservations & Preferences

I'd like to reserve a table...	**Chciałbym m /Chciałabym f zarezerwować stolik...** *hch'yahw•byhm/hch'yah•wah•byhm zah•reh•zehr•voh•vahch' stoh•leek...*
for two	**dla dwóch osób** *dlah dvooh oh•soop*
for this evening	**na dziś wieczór** *nah dj'eesh' vyeh•choor*
for tomorrow at...	**na jutro na...** *nah yoot•roh nah...*
A table for two, please.	**Proszę stolik dla dwóch osób.** _proh_•sheh _stoh_•leek dlah dvooh oh•soop
I have a reservation.	**Mam rezerwację.** mahm reh•zehr•_vahts_•yeh
My name is...	**Nazywam się...** nah•_zyh_•vahm sh'yeh...
Can we sit...?	**Możemy usiąść...?** moh•_zheh_•myh _oo_•sh'yohn'sh'ch'...
here/there	**tu/tam** too/tahm
outside	**na zewnątrz** nah _zehv_•nohntsh
in a non-smoking area	**w części dla niepalących** _fchehnsh'_•ch'ee dlah n'yeh•pah•_lohn_•tsyhh
by the window	**przy oknie** pshyh _ohk_•n'yeh
in the shade	**w cieniu?** _fch'yeh_•n'yoo
in the sun	**w słońcu?** _fswhon'_•tsoo
Where are the toilets?	**Gdzie są toalety?** gdj'yeh sohm toh•ah•_leh_•tyh

YOU MAY HEAR...

Czy ma pan rezerwację? chyh mah pahn reh•zehr•_vahts_•yeh	Do you have a reservation?
Dla ilu osób? dlah _ee_•loo oh•soop	For how many?
Co podać? tsoh _poh_•dahch'	What would you like?
Polecam... poh•_leh_•tsahm...	I recommend...
Smacznego. smahch•_neh_•goh	Enjoy your meal.

How to Order

Excuse me!	**Przepraszam!** psheh·_prah_·shahm
I'm ready to order.	**Chciałbym** m /**Chciałabym** f już zamówić. _hch'yahw_·byhm/_hch'yah_·wah·byhm yoosh zah·_moo_·veech'
May I see the wine list?	**Mogę prosić kartę win?** _moh_·geh _proh_·sheech' _kahr_·teh veen
I'd like...	**Poproszę...** poh·_proh_·sheh...
a bottle of...	**butelkę...** boo·_tehl_·keh...
a carafe of...	**karafkę...** kah·_rahf_·keh...
a glass of wine	**kieliszek wina** kyeh·_lee_·shehk _vee_·nah
a glass of water	**szklankę wody** _shklahn_·keh _voh_·dyh
Can I have a menu?	**Mogę prosić menu?** _moh_·geh _proh_·sh'eech' meh·_n'e_
Do you have...?	**Czy mają państwo...?** chyh _mah_·yohm _pahn's_·tfoh...
a menu in English	**menu po angielsku** meh·_n'ee_ poh ahn·_gyehls_·koo
a fixed-price menu	**zestawy** zehs·_tah_·vyh
a children's menu	**dania dla dzieci** _dah_·n'yah dlah _dj'yeh_·ch'ee
What do you recommend?	**Co może pan polecić?** tsoh _moh_·zheh pahn poh·_leh_·ch'eech'
What's this?	**Co to jest?** tso toh yehst
What's in it?	**Z czego to jest zrobione?** _scheh_·goh toh yehst zroh·_byoh_·neh
Is it spicy?	**Czy to jest ostre?** chyh toh yehst _oh_·streh
I'd like...	**Poproszę...** poh·_proh_·sheh...
More...please.	**Poproszę więcej...** poh·_proh_·sheh vyehn·tsehy...
With/Without...please.	**Poproszę z/bez...** poh·_proh_·sheh z/behs...
I can't eat...	**Nie mogę jeść...** n'yeh _moh_·geh yehsh'ch'...
rare	**krwisty** _krfees_·tyh
medium	**średnio wysmażony** _sh'rehd_·n'yoh vyhs·mah·_zhoh_·nyh

well-done	**dobrze wysmażony** _dohb_·zheh vyhs·mah·_zhoh_·nyh
It's to go [take away].	**Na wynos, poproszę.** nah _vyh_·nohs poh·_proh_·sheh
For Drinks, see page 76.	

YOU MAY SEE…

DANIA DNIA	menu of the day
OBSŁUGA (NIE)WLICZONA W CENĘ	service (not) included
SZEF KUCHNI POLECA	specials

Cooking Methods

baked	**pieczony** pyeh·_choh_·nyh
boiled	**gotowany** goh·toh·_vah_·nyh
braised	**duszony** doo·_shoh_·nyh
breaded	**panierowany** pah·n'yeh·roh·_vah_·nyh
creamed	**starty** _stahr_·tyh
diced	**pokrojony w kostkę** poh·kroh·_yoh_·nyh _fkohs_·tkeh
filleted	**filet** _fee_·leht
fried	**smażony** smah·_zhoh_·nyh
grilled	**grillowany** gree·loh·_vah_·nyh
poached	**z wody** _zvoh_·dyh
roasted	**pieczony** pyeh·_choh_·nyh
sautéed	**smażony sauté** smah·_zhoh_·nyh _soh_·teh
smoked	**wędzony** vehn·_dzoh_·nyh
steamed	**gotowany na parze** goh·toh·_vah_·nyh nah _pah_·zheh
stewed	**duszony** doo·_shoh_·nyh
stuffed	**faszerowany** fah·sheh·roh·vah·nyh

Dietary Requirements

I'm...	**Jestem...** _yehs_·tehm...
allergic to...	**uczulony na...** oo·choo·_loh_·nyh nah...
diabetic	**cukrzykiem** _yehs_·tehm tsook·_shyh_·kyehm
lactose intolerant.	**Mam nietolerancję laktozy.** mahm n'yeh·toh·leh·_rahn_·tsyeh lahk·_toh_·zyh
vegetarian	**wegetarianinem** _m_ /**wegetarianką** _f_ veh·geh·tahr·yah·_nee_·nehm/veg·geh·tah·_ryahn_·kohm
vegan	**weganinem** _m_ /**weganką** _f_ veh·gah·_nee_·nehm/ veh·_gahn_·kohm
I can't eat...	**Nie mogę jeść...** n'yeh _moh_·geh yehsh'ch'...
dairy products	**produktów mlecznych** proh·_dook_·toof _mlehch_·nyh
gluten	**glutenu** gloo·_teh_·noo
nuts	**orzechów** oh·_zheh_·hoof
pork	**wieprzowiny** vyehp·shoh·_vee_·nyh
shellfish	**owoców morza** oh·_voh_·tsoof _moh_·zhah
spicy food	**pikantnych potraw** pee·_kahnt_·nyhh _poht_·rahf
wheat	**pszenicy** psheh·_n'ee_·tsyh
Is it halal/kosher?	**Czy to jest halal/koszerne?** chyh toh yehst _hah_·lahl/koh·_shehr_·neh
Do you have...?	**Czy mają państwo...?** chyh _mah_·yohm _pahn's_·tfoh...
skimmed milk	**mleko odtłuszczone** _mleh_·koh ohd·twoosh·_choh_·ne
whole milk	**mleko pełne** _mleh_·koh _pehw_·neh
soya milk	**mleko sojowe** _mleh_·koh soh·_yoh_·veh

Dining With Children

Do you have children's portions?	**Mają państwo porcje dla dzieci?** _mah_·yohm _pahn's_·tfoh _pohr_·tsyeh dlah _dj'yeh_·ch'ee

Can I have a highchair/ child's seat?	**Mógłbym m /Mogłabym f dostać wysokie krzesełko/krzesełko dla dziecka?** _moogw•byhm/ moh•gwah•byhm dohs•tahch' vyh•soh•kyeh ksheh•sehw•koh/ksheh•sehw•koh dlah dj'yehts•kah_
Where can I feed/ change the baby?	**Gdzie mogę nakarmić/przewinąć dziecko?** _gdj'yeh moh•geh nah•kahr•meech'/psheh•vee•nohn'ch' dj'yehts•koh_
Can you warm this?	**Może pan to podgrzać?** _moh•zheh pahn toh pohd•gzhahch'_

For Traveling with Children, see page 146.

How to Complain

When will our food be ready?	**Jak długo jeszcze będziemy czekać na nasze zamówienie?** _yahk dwoo•goh yehsh•cheh behn•dj'yeh•myh cheh•kahch' nah nah•sheh zah•moo•vyeh•n'yeh_
We can't wait any longer.	**Nie możemy dłużej czekać.** _n'yeh moh•zheh•myh dwoo•zhehy cheh•kach'_
We're leaving.	**Wychodzimy.** _vyh•hoh•dj'ee•myh_
I didn't order this.	**Nie zamawiałem m /zamawiałam f tego.** _n'yeh zah•mah•vyah•wehm/zah•mah•vyah•wahm teh•goh_
I ordered…	**Zamawiałem m /Zamawiałam f…** _zah•mah•vyah•wehm/zah•mah•vyah•wahm…_
I can't eat this.	**Nie mogę tego jeść.** _n'yeh moh•geh teh•goh yehsh'ch'_
This is too…	**To jest za…** _toh yehst zah…_
cold/hot	**zimne/gorące** _zh'eem•neh/goh•rohn•tseh_
salty/spicy	**słone/ostre** _swoh•neh/ohs•treh_
tough/bland	**twarde/mdłe** _tfahr•deh/mdweh_
This isn't fresh.	**To jest nieświeże.** _toh yehst n'yeh•sh'fyeh•zheh_
This is dirty.	**To jest brudne.** _toh yehst brood•neh_

63

Paying

The check [bill], please.	**Poproszę rachunek.** *poh·proh·sheh rah·hoo·nehk*
Separate checks [bills], please.	**Chcielibyśmy zapłacić osobno.** *hch'yeh·lee·byhsh'·myh zah·pwah·ch'eech' oh·sohb·noh*
It's all together.	**Proszę policzyć wszystko razem.** *proh·sheh poh·lee·chyhch' fshyhst·koh rah·zehm*
Is service included?	**Czy obługa jest wliczona w cenę?** *chyh ohp·swoo·gah yehst vlee·choh·nah ftseh·neh*
What's this amount for?	**Za co jest ta kwota?** *zah tsoh yehst tah kfoh·tah*
I didn't have that.	**Nie jadłem m / jadłam f tego** *n'yeh yahd·wehm/ yahd·wahm teh·goh*
I had...	**Zjadłem m / zjadłam f ...** *zyahd·wehm/ zyahd·wahm ...*
Can I pay by credit card?	**Można płacić kartą kredytową?** *mohzh·nah pwah·ch'eech' kahr·tohm kreh·deeh·toh·vohm*
Can I have an itemized bill/a receipt?	**Czy mogę dostać szczegółowy rachunek/ pokwitowanie?** *chyh moh·geh dohs·tahch' shcheh·goo·woh·vyh rah·hoo·nehk/ pohk·fee·toh·vah·n'yeh*
That was delicious.	**Bardzo mi smakowało.** *bahr·dzoh mee smah·koh·vah·woh*
I've already paid	**Już zapłaciłem m /zapłaciłam f.** *yoosh zah·pwah·ch'ee·wehm/zah·pwah·ch'ee·wahm*

It is customary to tip your server 10% of the total bill. In more expensive restaurants the head waiter should also be tipped.

Meals & Cooking

Traditional Polish cuisine was influenced by the climate and location of Poland. Many dishes owe much to neighboring Russia, Germany and Hungary. Heavy soup, meat with root and/or pickled vegetables, cabbage, preserved fruit and dry and pickled mushrooms are still popular. So too are dumpling and noodle dishes. Modern Polish cuisine offers imaginative, healthy derivatives of traditional dishes. Salads and healthy snacks are popular, and vegetarian dishes are now common in restaurants.

Breakfast

boczek _boh_·chehk	bacon
bułki _boow_·kee	rolls
chleb hlehp	bread
dżem djehm	jam
herbata hehr·_bah_·tah	tea
jajecznica yah·yehch·_n'ee_·tsah	scrambled eggs
jajka sadzone _yahy_·kah sah·_dzoh_·neh	fried eggs

jajko na twardo/miękko _yahy_·koh nah _tfahr_·doh/_myehnk_·koh   hard-boiled/soft-boiled egg

jogurt _yoh_·goort   yogurt

kawa _kah_·vah   coffee

marmolada mahr·moh·_lah_·dah   marmalade

masło _mahs_·woh   butter

miód myoot   honey

mleko _mleh_·koh   milk

omlet _ohm_·leht   omelet

parówki pah·_roof_·kee   sausage

płatki śniadaniowe _pwaht_·kee shn'yah·dah·n'yoh·veh   cereal

ser sehr   cheese

tost tohst   toast

woda _voh_·dah   water

Śniadanie (breakfast) is usually served between 07:00 and 10:00 a.m. **Obiad** (lunch) is the main meal, traditionally enjoyed between 1:00 and 5:00 p.m., but with changing working habits more and more people have their main meal in the evening. **Kolacja** (supper) is typically served from 6:00 p.m. onwards.

Appetizers

grillowany oscypek gree·_loh_·vah·nyh ohs·_tsyh_·pehk   grilled and smoked ewe's milk cheese

grzybki marynowane _gzhyhp_·kee mah·ryh·noh·_vah_·neh   marinated wild mushrooms

naleśniki z kapustą i grzybami nah·lehsh'·_n'ee_·kee skah·_poos_·tohm ee gzhyh·_bah_·mee   thin pancakes with sauerkraut and mushrooms

pieczarki w śmietanie *pyeh·chahr·kee fsh'myeh·tah·n'yeh* — mushrooms in a cream sauce

sałatka *sah·waht·kah* — mixed salad

sałatka jarzynowa *sah·waht·kah yah·zhyh·noh·vah* — mixed vegetable salad in mayonnaise

sałatka pomidorowa z cebulą *sah·waht·kah poh·mee·doh·roh·vah stseh·boo·lohm* — tomato and onion salad

sałatka ziemniaczana *sah·waht·kah zh'yehm·n'yah·chah·nah* — potato salad

śledź w oleju *sh'lehdj' voh·leh·yoo* — herring in oil

śledź w śmietanie *sh'lehch' fsh'myeh·tah·n'yeh* — herring in sour cream

węgorz wędzony *vehn·gohsh vehn·dzoh·nyh* — smoked eel

Soup

barszcz czerwony *bahrshch chehr·voh·nyh* — beet soup

bulion z pasztecikiem *bool·yohn spahsh·teh·chee·kyehm* — consommé with meat-filled pastries

chłodnik z botwinki *hwohd·n'eek sboht·feen·kee* — a cold soup with sour cream, beets and dill, served with boiled eggs

grochówka *groh·hoof·kah* — pea soup

jarzynowa *yah·zhyh·noh·vah* — vegetable soup

kapuśniak *kah·poo·sh'·n'yahk* — sauerkraut soup

ogórkowa *oh·goor·koh·vah* — pickled cucumber soup

pomidorowa z ryżem/makaronem *poh·mee·doh·roh·vah z ryh·zhehm/mah·kah·roh·nehm* — tomato soup with rice/noodles

rosół (z kury) *roh·soow (skoo·ryh)* — (chicken) broth

szczawiowa *shchah·vyoh·vah* — sorrel soup with boiled eggs

żurek (z białą kiełbasą) *zhoo·rehk (zbyah·whom kyehw·bah·sohm)* — sour rye soup (with white sausage)

Fish & Seafood

dorsz *dohrsh*	cod
flądra *flohn·drah*	flounder [plaice]
homar *hoh·mahr*	lobster
karp *kahrp*	carp
karp po żydowsku *kahrp poh zhyh·doh·skoo*	carp Jewish style: seasoned and cooked in beer
karp smażony *kahrp smah·zhoh·nyh*	fried carp
krewetki *kreh·veht·kee*	shrimp [prawns]
leszcz *lehshch*	bream
łosoś *woh·sohsh'*	salmon
łupacz *woo·pahch'*	haddock
makrela *mahk·reh·lah*	mackerel
owoce morza *oh·voh·tseh moh·zhah*	seafood
pstrąg *pstrohnk*	trout
rak *rahk*	crayfish
ryba *ryh·bah*	fish
sandacz *sahn·dahch*	perch
sandacz po polsku *sahn·dahch poh pohls·koo*	perch in vegetable stock served with boiled eggs
śledź *sh'lehch'*	herring
szczupak (faszerowany) *shchoo·pahk (fah·sheh·roh·vah·nyh)*	(stuffed) pike
tuńczyk *toon'·chyhk*	tuna
węgorz *vehn·gohsh*	eel

Meat & Poultry

baranina *bah·rah·n'eeh·nah*	mutton
bigos *bee·gohs*	sauerkraut with meat, prunes and mushrooms
boczek *boh·chehk*	bacon

cielęcina ch'yeh·lehn'·ch'ee·nah		veal
drób droop		poultry
gęś gehn'sh'		goose
gołąbki goh·wohmp·kee		cabbage leaves stuffed with ground meat and rice
golonka goh·lohn·kah		pork shank
gulasz wieprzowy goo·lahsh vyehp·shoh·vyh		chopped pork with onions, pepper, garlic and tomato purée
indyk een·dyhk		turkey
jagnię yahg·n'yeh		lamb
kaczka kahch·kah		duck
kaczka pieczona z jabłkami kahch·kah pyeh·choh·nah zyahp·kah·mee		roast duck with apples
kiełbasa kyehw·bah·sah		sausage
klopsy klohp·syh		meatballs
kluski śląskie kloos·kee sh'lohns·kyeh		Silesian dumplings
kotlety schabowe koht·leh·tyh s·hah·boh·veh		breaded pork chops
kurczak koor·chahk		chicken
mięso myehn·soh		meat
ozór oh·zoor		tongue
pierogi z... pyeh·roh·gee z...		dumplings stuffed with...
mięsem myehn·sehm		meat
schab pieczony ze śliwkami s·hahp pyeh·choh·nyh zeh sh'leef·kah·mee		roast pork loin with prunes
stek stehk		steak
szynka shyhn·kah		ham
wieprzowina vyehp·shoh·vee·nah		pork
wołowina voh·woh·vee·nah		beef
zrazy zrah·zyh		rolled beef fillets

Vegetables & Staples

bakłażan *bahk·wah·zhahn*	eggplant [aubergine]
brokuł *broh·koow*	broccoli
brukselka *brook·sehl·kah*	Brussel sprout
burak *boo·rahk*	beet
cebula *tseh·boo·lah*	onion
cukinia *tsoo·kee·n'yah*	zucchini [courgette]
czosnek *chohs·nehk*	garlic
fasolka szparagowa *fah·sohl·kah shpah·rah·goh·vah*	green bean
groszek *groh·shehk*	pea
jarzyna *yah·zhyh·nah*	vegetable
kalafior *kah·lah·fyohr*	cauliflower
kapusta *kah·poos·tah*	cabbage
knedle ze śliwkami *knehd·leh zeh sh'leef·kah·mee*	dumplings stuffed with plums
leniwe pierogi *leh·n'ee·veh pyeh·roh·gee*	large dumplings made with flour, potatoes and curd cheese
marchew *mahr·hehf*	carrot
mieszane jarzyny *myeh·shah·neh yah·zhyh·nyh*	mixed vegetables

ogórek *oh-goo-rehk*		cucumber
papryka *pahp-ryh-kah*		pepper
pieczarka/grzyb *pyeh-chahr-kah/gzhyhb*		mushroom/wild mushroom
pierogi z... *pyeh-roh-gee z...*		dumplings stuffed with...
grzybami *gzhyh-bah-mee*		mushrooms
kapustą *kah-poos-tohm*		sauerkraut
serem *seh-rehm*		curd cheese
owocami *oh-voh-tsah-mee*		fruit
pierogi ruskie *pyeh-roh-gee roos-kyeh*		potato and curd cheese dumplings
placki ziemniaczane *plahts-kee zyehm-n'yah-chah-neh*		potato pancakes
pomidor *poh-mee-dohr*		tomato
rzepa *zheh-pah*		turnip
sałata *sah-wah-tah*		lettuce
seler naciowy *seh-lehr nah-ch'yoh-vyh*		celery
ziemniak *z'yehm-n'yahk*		potato
chleb *hlehp*		bread
ryż *ryhsh*		rice
mąka (pszenna) *mohn-kah (pshehn-nah)*		(wheat) flour
makaron *mah-kah-rohn*		pasta
cukier *tsoo-kyehr*		sugar

Fruit

agrest *ahg-rehst*		gooseberry
ananas *ah-nah-nahs*		pineapple
arbuz *ahr-boos*		watermelon
banan *bah-nahn*		banana
brzoskwinia *bzhohs-kfee-n'yah*		peach
cytryna *tsyh-tryh-nah*		lemon
czereśnia *cheh-resh'-n'yah*		cherry

grejpfrut _grehyp_·froot	grapefruit
jabłko _yahp_·koh	apple
limonka lee·_mohn_·kah	lime
malina mah·_lee_·nah	raspberry
morela mo·_reh_·lah	apricot
owoce oh·_voh_·tseh	fruit
pomarańcza poh·mah·_rahn'_·chah	orange
porzeczka czarna/czerwona poh·_zhech_·kah _chahr_·nah/chehr·_voh_·nah	black/red currant
śliwka _sh'leef_·kah	plum
truskawka troos·_kahf_·kah	strawberry
winogrono vee·noh·_groh_·noh	grape

Cheese

biały ser _byah_·wyh sehr	cottage cheese
bryndza _bryhn_·dzah	ewe's milk cheese
camembert kah·_mehm_·behr	camembert
ser sehr	cheese
ser pleśniowy sehr plehsh'·_n'yoh_·vyh	blue cheese
ser topiony _seh_·ryh tohp·_yoh_·nyh	processed cheese
ser żółty _seh_·ryh _zhoow_·tyh	hard cheese
twarożek tfah·_roh_·zhehk	curd cheese

Dessert

deser _deh_·sehr	dessert
galaretka z bitą śmietaną gah·lah·_reht_·kah _zbee_·tohm sh'myeh·_tah_·nohm	fruit jelly with whipped cream
gruszki w syropie _groosh_·kee fsyh·_roh_·pyeh	pears in syrup
kompot owocowy _kohm_·poht oh·voh·_tsoh_·vyh	fruit compote
lody... _loh_·dyh...	...ice cream
czekoladowe cheh·koh·lah·_doh_·veh	chocolate
malinowe mah·lee·_noh_·veh	raspberry

pistacjowe *pees·tats·yoh·veh*		pistachio
śmietankowe *sh'myeh·tahn·koh·veh·*		cream flavored
truskawkowe *troos·kahf·koh·veh*		strawberry
waniliowe *vah·n'eel·yoh·veh*		vanilla
murzynek *moo·zhyh·nek*		chocolate cake with chocolate icing
naleśniki *nah·lesh·n'ee·kee*		thin pancakes
owoce z bitą śmietaną *oh·voh·tseh zbee·tohm sh'myeh·tah·nohm*		fruit with whipped cream
racuchy z jabłkami *rah·tsoo·hyh z yahp·kah·mee*		small fried pancakes made with sliced apples
sernik *sehr·n'eek*		cheesecake
szarlotka *shahr·loht·kah*		apple tart

Sauces & Condiments

keczup *keh·choop*	ketchup
majonez *mah·yoh·nehs*	mayonaise
musztarda *moosh·tahr·dah*	mustard
oliwa *oh·lee·vah*	oil
pieprz *pyehpsh*	pepper
sól *sool*	salt
ocet *oh·tseht*	vinegar

At the Market

Where are the carts [trolleys]/baskets?	**Gdzie są wózki/koszyki?** *gdj'yeh sohm voos·kee/ koh·shyh·kee*
Where is/are…?	**Gdzie jest/są…?** *gdj'yeh yehst/sohm…*
I'd like some of that/ this…	**Poproszę trochę tego/tamtego…** *poh·proh·sheh troh·heh teh·goh/tahm·teh·goh…*
Can I taste it?	**Mogę spróbować?** *moh·geh sproo·boh·vahch'*
More/Less.	**Trochę więcej/mniej.** *troh·heh vyehn·tsehy/mn'yehy*
How much?	**Ile to kosztuje?** *ee·leh toh kohsh·too·yeh*

I'd like...	**Poproszę...** *poh·proh·sheh...*
a kilo/half-kilo of...	**kilo/pół kilo...** *kee·loh/poow kee·loh...*
a liter/half-liter of...	**litr/pół litra...** *leetr/poow leet·rah...*
a piece of...	**kawałek...** *kah·vah·wehk...*
a slice of...	**plasterek...** *plahs·teh·rehk...*
Where do I pay?	**Gdzie się płaci?** *gdj'yeh sh'yeh pwah·ch'ee*
A bag, please.	**Poproszę torbę.** *poh·proh·sheh tohr·beh*
I'm being helped.	**Już jestem obsługiwany m /**
	obsługiwana f . *joosh yehs·tehm*
	ohp·swoo·gee·vah·nyh/ohp·swoo·gee·vah·nah

For Conversion Tables, see page 176.

YOU MAY HEAR...

Czym mogę służyć? *chyhm moh·geh swoo·zhyhch'*	Can I help you?
Co dla pana? *tsoh dlah pah·nah*	What would you like?
Coś jeszcze? *tsohsh' yehsh·cheh*	Anything else?
To wszystko? *toh fshyhs·tkoh*	Is that all?
(To będzie)...złotych. *(toh behn·dj'yeh)... zwoh·tyhh*	(That's)...zlotys.

Measurements in Europe are metric — and that applies to the weight of food too. If you tend to think in pounds and ounces, it's worth brushing up on what the metric equivalent is before you go shopping for fruit and veg in markets and supermarkets. Five hundred grams, or half a kilo, is a common quantity to order, and that converts to just over a pound (17.65 ounces, to be precise).

YOU MAY SEE...

NAJLEPIEJ SPOŻYĆ PRZED...	best if used by...
KALORIE	calories
BEZ TŁUSZCZU	fat free
PRZECHOWYWAĆ W LODÓWCE	keep refrigerated
MOŻE ZAWIERAĆ ŚLADOWE ILOŚCI...	may contain traces of...
SPRZEDAĆ PRZED	sell by

In the Kitchen

bottle opener	**otwieracz do butelek** oht·_fyeh_·rahch doh boo·_teh_·lehk
bowl	**miska** _mees_·kah
can opener	**otwieracz do puszek** oht·_fyeh_·rahch doh _poo_·shehk
corkscrew	**korkociąg** kohr·_koh_·ch'yohnk
cup	**filiżanka** fee·lee·_zhahn_·kah
fork	**widelec** vee·_deh_·lehts
frying pan	**patelnia** pah·_tehl_·n'yah
glass (non-alcoholic/ alcoholic)	**szklanka/kieliszek** _shklahn_·kah/kyeh·_lee_·shehk
knife	**nóż** noosh
measuring cup/spoon	**miarka kuchenna/łyżka do odmierzania** _myahr_·kah koo·_hehn_·nah/_wyhsh_·kah doh ohd·myeh·_zhah_·n'yah
napkin	**serwetka** sehr·_veht_·kah
plate	**talerz** _tah_·lehsh
pot	**garnek** _gahr_·nehk
saucepan	**rondel** _rohn_·dehl
spatula	**łopatka** woh·_paht_·kah
spoon	**łyżka** _wyhsh_·kah
teaspoon	**łyżeczka** wyh·_zhehch'_·kah

Drinks

ESSENTIAL

Can I see the wine list/ drink menu?	**Czy mogę prosić kartę win/listę drinków?** *chyh moh•geh proh•sheech' kahr•teh veen/lees•teh dreen•koof*
What do you recommend?	**Co może pan polecić?** *tsoh moh•zheh pahn poh•leh•ch'eech'*
I'd like a bottle/glass of red/white wine.	**Poproszę butelkę/kieliszek czerwonego/białego wina.** *poh•proh•sheh boo•tehl•keh/kyeh•lee•shehk chehr•voh•neh•goh/byah•weh•goh vee•nah*
The house wine, please.	**Poproszę wino stołowe.** *poh•proh•sheh vee•noh stoh•woh•veh*
Another bottle/glass, please.	**Poproszę jeszcze jedną butelkę/jeden kieliszek.** *poh•proh•sheh yehsh•cheh jehd•nohm boo•tehl•keh/yeh•dehn kyeh•lee•shehk*
I'd like a local beer.	**Poproszę lokalne piwo.** *poh•proh•sheh loh•kahl•neh pee•voh*

Can I buy you a drink?	**Mogę postawić panu drinka?** _moh_·geh	
	pohs·tah·veech' pah·noo dreen·kah	
Cheers!	**Na zdrowie!** _nah zdroh·vyeh_	
A coffee/tea, please.	**Poproszę kawę/herbatę.** _poh·proh·sheh kah·veh/_	
	hehr·bah·teh	
Black	**Czarną** _chahr·nohm_	
A coffee with…, please.	**Poproszę kawę z…** _poh·proh·sheh kah·veh z…_	
milk	**mlekiem** _mleh·kyehm_	
sugar	**cukrem** _tsook·rehm_	
artificial sweetener	**słodzikiem** _swoh·dj'ee·kyehm_	
I'd like…	**Poproszę…** _poh·proh·sheh…_	
a juice	**sok** _sohk_	
a cola	**colę** _koh·leh_	
a (sparkling/still) water	**wodę (gazowaną/niegazowaną)** _voh·deh_	
	(gah·zoh·vah·nohm/n'yeh·gah·zoh·vah·nohm)	
Is the tap water safe to drink?	**Można pić wodę z kranu?** _mohzh·nah peech'_	
	voh·deh skrah·noo	

Non-alcoholic Drinks

cola _koh·lah_	cola
gorąca czekolada _goh·rohn·tsah cheh·koh·lah·dah_	hot chocolate
herbata… _hehr·bah·tah…_	tea…
czarna _chahr·nah_	black
owocowa _oh·voh·tsoh·vah_	fruit
zielona _zh'yeh·loh·nah_	green
ziołowa _zh'yoh·woh·vah_	herbal
z cukrem _stsook·rehm_	with sugar
z cytryną _stsyht·ryh·nohm_	with lemon

kawa... _kah·vah..._		coffee...
z mlekiem _zmleh·kyehm_		with milk
z cukrem _stsook·rehm_		with sugar
czarna _chahr·nah_		black
bezkofeinowa _behs·koh·feh·ee·noh·vah_		decaffeinated
z ekspresu _zehks·preh·soo_		espresso
po turecku _poh too·rehts·koo_		Turkish
lemoniada _leh·moh·n'yah·dah_		lemonade
mleko _mleh·koh_		milk
shake _shehyk_		milk shake
sok... _sohk..._		...juice
grejpfrutowy _grehyp·froo·toh·vyh_		grapefruit
pomarańczowy _poh·mah·rahn'·choh·vyh_		orange
jabłkowy _yahp·koh·vyh_		apple
owocowy _sohk oh·voh·tsoh·vyh_		juice
świeżo wyciskany _sh'fyeh·zho_ _vyh·ch'ees·kah·nyh_		fresh squeezed
woda gazowana/niegazowana _voh·dah_ _gah·zoh·vah·nah/n'yeh·gah·zoh·vah·nah_		sparkling/still water

Tea is a popular beverage in Poland, usually enjoyed black or
with lemon. Traditionally, **esencja** (the essence) was brewed in
a small ceramic teapot over a boiling kettle. The essence was poured
into a glass or cup and boiling water was added. Nowadays, tea bags
are frequently used. Other types of tea, such as green, fruit or herbal
tea, have become increasingly popular. Coffee is also popular, and
many drink instant coffee at home. Specialty coffee, including espresso
and mocha, is available at many of the numerous **kawiarnie** (coffee
shops) in town.

YOU MAY HEAR...

Czy mogę postawić panu coś do picia?
chyh moh·geh pohs·tah·vich' pah·noo tsosh' doh pee·ch'yah
Can I get you a drink?

Z mlekiem i z cukrem? *z mleh·kyehm ee stsook·rehm*
With milk and sugar?

Gazowana czy niegazowana?
gah·zoh·vah·nah chyh n'yeh gah·zoh·vah·nah
Sparkling or still water?

Aperitifs, Cocktails & Liqueurs

ajerkoniak *ah·yehr·koh·n'yahk*	egg-yolk liqueur
gin *djeen*	gin
koniak *koh·n'yahk*	imported brandy
miód pitny *myoot peet·nyh*	mead
szarlotka *shahr·loht·kah*	grass-flavored vodka and apple juice
śliwowica *sh'lee·voh·vee·tsah*	plum brandy
whisky *wees·kee*	whisky
winiak *vee·n'yahk*	Polish brandy
wódka... *voot·kah...*	vodka...
czysta *chyhs·tah*	straight [neat]
z lodem *z loh·dehm*	on the rocks [with ice]
z wodą/tonikiem *z voh·dohm/ toh·n'ee·kyehm*	with water/tonic water
żubrówka *zhoob·roof·kah*	vodka flavored with bison grass

Vodka is one of the best known Polish exports. Several brands, such as Chopin® and Sobieski®, are very popular in the U.S. and U.K. However, the greatest Polish specialty is Żubrówka®, vodka flavored with a unique grass growing only in **Puszcza Białowieska** (Białowieża Forest) in eastern Poland. The grass lends Bison Vodka its unmistakeable taste and characteristic yellowish color. Vodka is served cold and enjoyed from small glasses or mixed with juice or soda. Flavored vodka is also popular.

Vodka, made from either potatoes or rye, is still the national drink, but beer has recently become equally popular.

Polish beer includes Żywiec™, Tyskie™, Lech™ and Warka™; most well-known international brands can also be found.

Beer

piwo... _pee·voh..._	beer...
bezalkoholowe _behz·ahl·koh·hoh·loh·veh_	non-alcoholic
butelkowe/beczkowe _boo·tehl·koh·veh/ behch·koh·veh_	bottled/draft [draught]
ciemne/jasne _ch'yehm·neh/yahs·neh_	dark/light
jasne pełne _yahs·neh pehw·neh_	lager
lokalne _loh·kahl·neh_	local
pilsner _peel·znehr_	pilsner

Wine

wino... _vee·noh..._	...wine
białe _byah·weh_	white
czerwone _chehr·voh·neh_	red
deserowe _deh·seh·roh·veh_	dessert
musujące _moo·soo·yohn·tseh_	sparkling

On the Menu

ajerkoniak *ah·yehr·koh·n'yahk* liqueur made from egg yolks, aromatic spirits, sugar, vanilla and brandy

agrest *ahg·rehst* gooseberry

alkohol *ahl·koh·hohl* alcohol

ananas *ah·nah·nahs* pineapple

arbuz *ahr·boos* watermelon

awokado *ah·voh·kah·doh* avocado

babeczka *bah·behch·kah* scone

bakłażan *bahk·wah·zhahn* eggplant [aubergine]

banan *bah·nahn* banana

baranina *bah·rah·n'ee·nah* mutton

baranina pieczona ze śmietaną *bah·rah·n'ee·nah pyeh·choh·nah zeh sh'myeh·tah·nohm* roast mutton with sour cream

barszcz (czerwony) *bahrshch (chehr·voh·nyh)* (red) beet [beetroot] soup

bażant *bah·zhahnt* pheasant

bazylia *bah·zyhl·yah* basil

befsztyk tatarski *behf·shtyhk tah·tahrs·kee* steak tartare

beza *beh·zah* meringue

bezkofeinowa *behs·koh·feh·ee·<u>noh</u>·vah*	decaffeinated
biała kapusta *<u>byah</u>·wah kah·<u>poos</u>·tah*	white cabbage
białko *<u>byahw</u>·koh*	egg white
biały ser *<u>byah</u>·wyh sehr*	cottage cheese
bigos *<u>bee</u>·gohs*	sauerkraut with slices of meat, pork sausage, prunes and mushrooms
biszkopt *<u>beesh</u>·kohpt*	sponge cake
bita śmietana *<u>bee</u>·tah sh'myeh·<u>tah</u>·nah*	whipped cream
boczek *<u>boh</u>·chehk*	bacon
brokuł *<u>broh</u>·koow*	broccoli
brukiew *<u>broo</u>·kyehf*	rutabaga [swede]
brukselka *brook·<u>sehl</u>·kah*	Brussels sprout
bryndza *<u>bryhn</u>·dzah*	ewe's milk cheese
brzoskwinia *bzhohs·<u>kfee</u>·n'yah*	peach
budyń *<u>boo</u>·dyhn'*	pudding
budyń z karmelem *<u>boo</u>·dyhn' skahr·<u>meh</u>·lehm*	caramel pudding
bulion *<u>boo</u>·lyohn*	clear soup
bułka *<u>boow</u>·kah*	roll
bułka tarta *<u>boow</u>·kah <u>tahr</u>·tah*	bread crumbs
burak *<u>boo</u>·rahk*	beet [beetroot]
cebula *tseh·<u>boo</u>·lah*	onion
chipsy *<u>cheep</u>·syh*	chips [crisps]
chleb *hlehp*	bread
chleb pszenny *hlehp <u>pshehn</u>·nyh*	wheat bread
chleb razowy *hlehp rah·<u>zoh</u>·vyh*	whole-wheat [wholemeal] bread
chleb żytni *hlehp <u>zhyht</u>·nee*	rye bread
chłodnik *<u>hwohd</u>·n'eek*	cold yogurt, dill and beet [beetroot] soup
chrupki *<u>hroop</u>·kee*	corn snacks

chrzan *hshahn*	horseradish
ciasteczko *ch'yahs•tehch•koh*	cookie [biscuit]
ciasto *ch'yahs•toh*	pastry, cake
ciasto francuskie *ch'yahs•toh frahn•tsoos•kyeh*	puff pastry
ciasto z bakaliami *ch'yahs•toh zbah•kahl•yah•mee*	dried fruit cake
ciecierzyca *ch'yeh•ch'yeh•zhyh•tsah*	chick pea
cielęcina *ch'yeh•lehn'•ch'ee•nah*	veal
comber *cohm•behr*	loin (usually game)
cukier *tsoo•kyehr*	sugar
cukinia *tsoo•kee•n'yah*	zucchini [courgette]
ćwikła *ch'feek•wah*	horseradish with beets [beetroot]
cykoria *tsyh•koh•ryah*	endive
cynamon *tsyh•nah•mohn*	cinnamon
cytryna *tsyh•tryh•nah*	lemon
czarna *chahr•nah*	black (coffee)
czarna porzeczka *chahr•nah poh•zhehch•kah*	black currant
czarny chleb *czahr•nyh hlehp*	dark bread
czekolada *cheh•koh•lah•dah*	chocolate
czereśnia *cheh•rehsh•n'yah*	cherry
czerwona fasola *chehr•voh•nah fah•soh•lah*	kidney bean
czerwona kapusta *chehr•voh•nah kah•poos•tah*	red cabbage
czerwone *chehr•voh•neh*	red (wine)
czerwony pieprz *cher•voh•nyh pyehpsh*	chilli pepper
czosnek *chohs•nehk*	garlic
daktyl *dahk•tyhl*	date
deser *deh•sehr*	dessert
domowy *doh•moh•vyh*	homemade
dorsz *dohrsh*	cod
drink *dreenk*	alcoholic drink

drób *droop*	poultry
dymka _dyhm_·kah	spring onion
dynia *dyh*·n'yah	pumpkin
dżem *djehm*	jam
dziczyzna *dj'ee*·_chyhz_·nah	game
dzik *dj'eek*	wild boar
estragon *ehs*·_trah_·gohn	tarragon
fasola *fah*·_soh_·lah	bean
fasolka szparagowa *fah*·_sohl_·kah _shpah_·rah·_goh_·vah	green bean
figa suszona/świeża _fee_·gah soo·_shoh_·nah/ _sh'vyeh_·zhah	dried/fresh fig
flądra _flohn_·drah	flounder [plaice]
flaki _flah_·kee	tripe
frytki _fryht_·kee	French fries [chips]
galaretka *gah*·lah·_reht_·kah	jelly
gałka muszkatołowa _gaw_·kah moosh·kah·toh·_woh_·vah	nutmeg
gęś *gehn'sh'*	goose
gęsty _gehns_·tyh	rich (sauce)
gin z tonikiem *djeen stoh*·_nee_·kyehm	gin and tonic
głowizna *gwoh*·_veez_·nah	pig's head [brawn]
gołąbki *goh*·_whomp_·kee	ground [minced] meat with rice rolled in cabbage leaves
golonka *goh*·_lohn_·kah	pork shank
gorąca czekolada *goh*·_rohn_·tsah cheh·koh·_lah_·dah	hot chocolate
gorzki _gohsh_·kee	bitter
goździki *gozh'*·_dj'ee_·kee	cloves
grejpfrut _greyp_·froot	grapefruit
grochówka *groh*·_hoof_·kah	pea soup

groszek _groh_·shehk — pea

groszek cukrowy _groh_·shehk tsook·_roh_·vyh — sugarsnap pea

gruszka _groosh_·kah — pear

gruszki w syropie _groosh_·kee fsyh·_roh_·pyeh — pears in syrup

grzane wino _gzhah_·neh _vee_·noh — mulled wine

grzyb gzhyhb — wild mushroom

gulasz goo·lahsh — meat stewed in gravy

gulasz wieprzowy goo·lahsh vyep·_shoh_·vyh — pork stew

gulasz z jagnięcia goo·lahsh zyahg·_nyehn'_·ch'yah — lamb stew

herbata hehr·_bah_·tah — tea

herbatnik hehr·_baht_·n'eek — biscuit

homar _hoh_·mahr — lobster

imbir _eem_·beer — ginger

indyk _een_·dyhk — turkey

jabłko _yahp_·koh — apple

jagnię _yahg_·n'yeh — lamb

jagoda yah·_goh_·dah — blueberry

jajecznica yah·yehch·_n'ee_·tsah — scrambled eggs

jajko _yahy_·koh — egg

jajko na miękko _yahy_·koh nah _myenk_·koh — soft-boiled egg

jajko na twardo _yahy_·koh nah _tfahr_·doh — hard-boiled egg

jajko sadzone _yahy_·koh sah·_dzoh_·neh — fried egg

jarzyna yah·_zhyh_·nah — vegetable

jeżyna yeh·_zhyh_·nah — blackberry

jogurt _yoh_·goort — yogurt

kabaczek kah·_bah_·chehk — marrow

kaczka _kahch_·kah — duck

kaczka pieczona z jabłkami _kahch_·kah pyeh·_choh_·nah z yahp·_kah_·mee — roast duck with apples

kalafior kah·_lah_·fyohr — cauliflower

kałamarnica *kah·wah·mahr·n'ee·tsah* — squid
kanapka *kah·nahp·kah* — sandwich
kapary *kah·pah·ryh* — capers
kapuśniak *kah·poosh'·n'yahk* — sauerkraut soup
kapusta *kah·poos·tah* — cabbage
kapusta kiszona *kah·poos·tah kee·shoh·nah* — sauerkraut
karczoch *kahr·chohh* — artichoke
karp *kahrp* — carp
karp po żydowsku *kahrp poh zhyh·dohs·koo* — carp with spices cooked in beer
karp smażony *kahrp smah·zhoh·nyh* — fried carp
kaszanka *kah·shahn·kah* — black pudding
kasztan *kahsh·tah·nyh* — chestnut (sweet)
kawa *kah·vah* — coffee
kawa rozpuszczalna *kah·vah rohs·poosh·chahl·nah* — instant coffee
kawior *kah·vyohr* — caviar
kefir *keh·feer* — thin yogurt
kiełbasa *kyehw·bah·sah* — sausage
kiełbaska wieprzowa *kyehw·bahs·kah vyehp·shoh·vah* — pork sausage
kiełek fasoli *kyeh·wehk fah·soh·lee* — bean sprout

kisiel _kee·sh'ehl_	jelly
kiwi _kee·vee_	kiwi
klops _klohps_	meatball
kluski _kloos·kee_	noodles, dumplings
kluski śląskie _kloos·kee sh'lohns·kyeh_	Silesian dumplings
kminek _kmee·nehk_	caraway
knedle ze śliwkami _knehd·leh zeh shleef·kah·mee_	dumplings stuffed with plums
kokos _koh·kohs_	coconut
kompot _kohm·poht_	stewed fruit
koper _koh·pehr_	fennel
koperek _koh·peh·rehk_	dill
kopytka _koh·pyht·kah_	small potato dumplings
korniszon _kohr·n'ee·shohn_	gherkin
kość _kohsh'ch'_	bone
kotlet _koht·leht_	chop
kotlet schabowy _koht·leht s·hah·boh·vyh_	pork chop fried and breaded
kozie mleko _koh·zh'yeh mleh·koh_	goat's milk
krab _krahp_	crab
krakers _krah·kehrs_	cracker
krewetka _kreh·veht·kah_	shrimp [prawn]
krokiet _kroh·kyeht_	croquette
królik _kroo·leek_	rabbit
krupnik _kroop·neek_	barley soup
kukurydza _koo·koo·ryh·dzah_	corn
kurczak _koor·chahk_	chicken
kurczak grillowany _koor·chahk gree·loh·vah·nyh_	grilled chicken
kurczak pieczony _koor·chahk pyeh·choh·nyh_	roast chicken
kurczak smażony _koor·chahk smah·zhoh·nyh_	fried chicken
kurka _koor·kah_	chanterelle mushroom

kuropatwa *koo·roh·paht·fah* — partridge

kwaśny *kfahsh'·nyh* — sour (taste)

łagodny *wah·gohd·neh* — mild (flavor)

langusta *lahn·goos·tah* — lobster

lekki *lehk·kee* — light (sauce)

lemoniada *leh·moh·n'yah·dah* — lemonade

leniwe pierogi *leh·n'ee·veh pyeh·roh·gee* — flour, potato and curd cheese dumplings

leszcz *lehshch* — bream

likier *lee·kyehr* — liqueur

limonka *lee·mohn·kah* — lime

liść laurowy *leesh'ch' lahw·roh·vyh* — bay leaf

lód *loot* — ice

lody *loh·dyh* — ice cream

łopatka *woh·paht·kah* — shoulder (cut of meat)

łosoś *woh·sohsh'* — salmon

łosoś wędzony *woh·sohsh' vehn·dzoh·nyh* — smoked salmon

lukier *loo·kyehr* — icing

łupacz *woo·pahch* — haddock

majonez *mah·yoh·nehs* — mayonnaise

majonez czosnkowy *mah·yoh·nehs chohsn·koh·vyh* — garlic mayonnaise

mąka *mohn·kah* — flour

mąka pszenna *mohn·kah pshehn·nah* — wheat flour

mąka razowa *mohn·kah rah·zoh·vah* — whole-wheat [wholemeal] flour

makaron *mah·kah·rohn* — pasta

makrela *mahk·reh·lah* — mackerel

malina *mah·lee·nah* — raspberry

małża *mahw·zhah* — mussel

mandarynka *mahn·dah·ryhn·kah* — tangerine

marcepan *mahr·tseh·pahn* marzipan
marchew *mahr·hehf* carrot
margaryna *mahr·gah·ryh·nah* margarine
marmolada *mahr·moh·lah·dah* marmalade
marynowany w occie *mah·ryh·noh·vah·nyh vohts·ch'yeh* marinated in vinegar
maślanka *mahsh'·lahn·kah* buttermilk
masło *mahs·woh* butter
mazurek *mah·zoo·rehk* Easter shortcake (various flavors)
melasa *meh·lah·sah* molasses [treacle]
melon *meh·lohn* melon
miecznik *myehch·n'eek* swordfish
mielona wołowina *myeh·loh·nah voh·woh·vee·nah* minced beef
mięso *myehn·soh* meat
mięso grillowane *myehn·soh gree·loh·vah·neh* grilled meat
mieszane jarzyny *myeh·shah·neh yah·zhyh·nyh* mixed vegetables
mięta *myehn·tah* mint
migdał *meeg·dahw* almond
migdały w cukrze *meeg·dah·wyh ftsook·sheh* sugared almonds
miód *myoot* honey
miód pitny *myoot peet·nyh* mead
mizeria *mee·zeh·ryah* cucumber salad with sour cream
mleko *mle·koh* milk
młoda kapusta *mwoh·dah kah·poos·tah* spring cabbage
młody kurczak *mwoh·dyh koor·chahk* spring chicken
mocne *mohyts·neh* full-bodied (wine), strong (beer)

morela *moh·reh·lah*	apricot
morwa *mohr·vah*	mulberry
mrożony *mroh·zhoh·nyh*	iced (drinks)
mus *moos*	mousse
musujący *moo·soo·yohn·tsyh*	sparkling
musztarda *moosh·tahr·dah*	mustard
naleśnik *nah·lehsh'·n'eek*	thin pancake
naleśniki z kapustą i grzybami *nah·lehsh'·n'ee·kee skah·poos·tohm ee gzhyh·bah·mee*	thin pancakes with sauerkraut and mushrooms
napój *nah·puy*	soft drink
nektarynka *nehk·tah·ryhn·kah*	nectarine
nerka *nehr·kah*	kidney
nerkówka *nehr·koof·kah*	loin (cut of meat)
noga *noh·gah*	leg (cut of meat)
nóżki *noosh·kee*	pigs' feet
nugat *noo·gaht*	nougat
ogon *oh·gohn*	oxtail
ogórek *oh·goo·rehk*	cucumber
ogórek kiszony *oh·goo·rehk kee·shoh·nyh*	dill pickle
ogórek konserwowy *oh·goo·rehk kohn·sehr·voh·vyh*	pickle
ogórkowa *oh·goor·koh·vah*	pickled cucumber soup
okoń *oh·kohn'*	bass
oliwka *oh·leef·kah*	olive
oliwki nadziewane *oh·leef·kee nah·dj'yeh·vah·neh*	stuffed olives
omlet *ohm·leht*	omelet
opieniek *oh·pyeh·n'yehk*	oyster mushroom
oranżada *oh·rahn·zhah·dah*	orangeade
orzech *oh·zhehh*	nut

orzech laskowy *oh·zhehh lahs·koh·vyh* — hazelnut

orzech nerkowca *oh·zhehh nehr·kohf·tsah* — cashew

orzech włoski *oh·zhehh vwohs·kee* — walnut

orzechy mieszane *oh·zheh·hyh myeh·shah·neh* — assorted nuts

orzeszek ziemny *oh·zheh·shehk zh'yehm·nyh* — peanut

orzeszki ziemne solone *oh·zhehsh·kee zh'yehm·neh soh·loh·neh* — salted peanuts

ośmiornica *ohsh'·myohr·nee·tsah* — octopus

ostra kiełbaska *ohs·trah kyehw·bahs·kah* — spicy sausage

ostry (smak) *ohs·tryh (smahk)* — hot, spicy (flavor)

ostryga *ohs·tryh·gah* — oyster

owoce *oh·voh·tseh* — fruit

owoce kandyzowane *oh·voh·tseh kahn·dyh·zoh·vah·neh* — candied fruit

owoce morza *oh·voh·tseh moh·zhah* — seafood

owoce z puszki *oh·voh·tseh spoosh·kee* — canned fruit

owsianka *ohf·sh'yahn·kah* — porridge

ozór *oh·zoor* — tongue

pączek *pohn·chehk* — donut [doughnut]

papryka zielona/czerwona *pahp·ryh·kah zh'yeh·loh·nah/chehr·voh·nah* — green/red pepper

parówka *pah·roof·kah* — sausage

pasternak *pah·stehr·nahk* — parsnip

paszteciki *pahsh·teh·ch'ee·kee* — pastries filled with meat, fish or cabbage

pasztet *pahsh·teht* — pâté

pasztet w galarecie *pahsh·teht vgah·lah·reh·ch'yeh* — pâté in aspic

perliczka *pehr·leech·kah* — guinea fowl

pieczarka *pyeh·chahr·kah* — mushroom

pieczarki w śmietanie *pyeh·chahr·kee vsh'myeh·tah·n'yeh* — mushrooms in cream

pieczeń *pyeh·chehn'* — pot roast

pieczona wołowina *pyeh·choh·nah voh·woh·vee·nah* — roast beef

pieprz *pyehpsh* — pepper (condiment)

pieprzny sos *pyehp·shnyh sohs* — hot pepper sauce

piernik *pyehr·n'eek* — ginger cake

pierogi *pyeh·roh·gee* — stuffed dumplings

pierogi ruskie *pyeh·roh·gee roos·kyeh* — dumplings with cheese and onion

pierogi z kapustą i z grzybami *pyeh·roh·gee skah·poos·tohm ee zgzhyh·bah·mee* — dumplings with sauerkraut and mushrooms

pierogi z mięsem *pyeh·roh·gee zmyehn·sehm* — dumplings with meat

pierogi z owocami *pyeh·roh·gee zoh·voh·tsah·mee* — dumplings with fruit

pierogi z serem *pyeh·roh·gee sseh·rehm* — dumplings with curd cheese

pierś *pyehrsh'* — breast

pierś z kurczaka *pyehrsh' skoor·chah·kah* — breast of chicken

pietruszka zielona *pyeht·roosh·kah zh'yeh·loh·nah* — parsley

pikantny *pee·kahnt·nyh* — spicy

piwo *pee·voh* — beer

piwo jasne pełne *pee·voh yahs·neh pehw·neh* — lager

placek *plah·tsehk* — tart, pie

placki ziemniaczane *plahts·kee zh'yehm·n'yah·chah·neh* — potato pancakes

płatki śniadaniowe *pwaht·kee sh'nyah·dah·n'yoh·veh* — cereal

podroby *pohd·roh·byh* — giblets

polędwica *poh·lehnd·vee·tsah* — tenderloin (cut of meat)

pomarańcza *poh·mah·rahn'·chah* — orange

pomidor *poh·mee·dohr* — tomato

pomidorowa z makaronem/ryżem — tomato soup with noodles/rice
poh·mee·doh·roh·vah z mah·kah·roh·nehm/ ryh·zhehm

poncz *pohnch* — punch

por *pohr* — leek

porcja *pohr·tsyah* — portion

porto *pohr·toh* — port

potrawa *poh·trah·vah* — dish

potrawka *poh·trahf·kah* — casserole

prosiak *proh·sh'yahk* — suckling pig

przekąski *psheh·kohns·kee* — snacks

przepiórka *psheh·pyoor·kah* — quail

przyprawy *pshyh·prah·vyh* — seasoning, spices

przysmak regionalny *pshyhs·mahk reh·gyoh·nahl·nyh* — local specialty

pstrąg *pstrohnk* — trout

purée *pee·reh* — purée

purée z ziemniaków *pee·reh zzh'yehm·n'yah·koof* — potato purée

pyzy *pyh·zyh* — large potato dumplings, sometimes with meat stuffing

rabarbar *rah·bahr·bahr* — rhubarb

racuch *rah·tsooh* — small pancake

racuchy z jabłkami *rah·tsoo·hyh zyahp·kah·mee* — apple pancakes, fritters

rak *rahk* — crayfish

rodzynki *roh·dzyhn·kee* — raisins

rolmops *rohl·mohps* — pickled herring filet [rollmop herring]

rosół _roh_•soow	consommé, broth
rosół z kury _roh_•soow skoo•ryh	chicken broth
rosół z mięsem i jarzynami _roh_•soow zmyehn•sehm ee yah•zhyh•_nah_•mee	meat and vegetable broth
rostbef _rohst_•behf	roast beef
rozmaryn rohz•_mah_•ryhn	rosemary
rumsztyk _room_•shtyhk	rumpsteak
ryba _ryh_•bah	fish
ryż rysh	rice
rzepa _zheh_•pah	turnip
rzeżucha zheh•_zhoo_•hah	cress
rzeżucha wodna zheh•_zhoo_•hah vohd•nah	watercress
rzodkiewka zhoht•_kyehf_•kah	radish
sałata sah•_wah_•tah	lettuce
sałatka jarzynowa sah•_waht_•kah yah•zhyh•_noh_•vah	mixed vegetable salad
sałatka z kapusty sah•_waht_•kah skah•_poos_•tyh	coleslaw
salceson sahl•_tseh_•sohn	headcheese [brawn]
sandacz _sahn_•dahch	perch
sandacz po polsku _sahn_•dahch poh _pohl_•skoo	perch in vegetable stock with eggs
sardela sahr•_deh_•lah	anchovy
sardynka sahr•_dyhn_•kah	sardine
sarnina sahr•_nee_•nah	venison
schab s•hahp	loin of pork
schab pieczony ze śliwkami s•hahp pyeh•_choh_•nyh zeh sh'leef•_kah_•mee	roast pork sirloin with prune
schłodzony s•hwoh•_dzoh_•nyh	chilled
seler naciowy _seh_•lehr nah•_ch'yoh_•vyh	celery
ser sehr	cheese
ser kozi sehr koh•_zh'ee_	goat's cheese

ser owczy *sehr ohf·chyh* — ewe's milk cheese

ser pleśniowy *sehr pleh·sh'n'yoh·vyh* — blue cheese

ser topiony *sehr toh·pyoh·nyh* — processed cheese

serce *sehr·tseh* — heart

sernik *sehr·n'eek* — cheesecake

shake *shehyk* — milkshake

śledź *sh'lehch'* — herring

śledź marynowany *sh'lehdj' mah·ryh·noh·vah·nyh* — marinated herring

śledź w oleju *sh'lehdj' voh·leh·yoo* — herring in oil

śledź w śmietanie *sh'lehch' fsh'myeh·tah·n'yeh* — herring in sour cream

ślimak *sh'lee·mahk* — snail

śliwka *sh'leef·kah* — plum

śliwowica *sh'lee·voh·vee·tsah* — plum brandy

słodka papryka *swoht·kah pah·pryh·kah* — sweet red pepper

słodki *swoht·kee* — sweet

słodycze *swoh·dyh·cheh* — candies [sweets]

słodzik *swoh·dj'eek* — sweetener

śmietana *sh'myeh·tah·nah* — cream

soczewica *soh·cheh·vee·tsah* — lentil

sok *sohk* — juice

sok cytrynowy *sohk tsyh·tryh·noh·vyh* — lemon juice

sok owocowy *sohk oh·voh·tsoh·vyh* — fruit juice

sok pomarańczowy *sohk poh·mah·ran'·choh·vyh* — orange juice

sok z limonki *sohk zlee·mohn·kee* — lime juice

sól *sool* — salt

sola *soh·lah* — sole

solony *soh·loh·nyh* — salted

sos *sohs* — sauce

sos czosnkowy *sohs chohsn·koh·vyh* — garlic sauce

sos pomidorowy *sohs poh•mee•doh•roh•vyh*	tomato sauce
sos słodko-kwaśny *sohs swoht•koh•kfahsh'•nyh*	sweet and sour sauce
sos winegret *sohs vee•neh•greh*	vinaigrette [French dressing]
sos z pieczeni *sohs spyeh•cheh•n'ee*	gravy
specjalność szefa kuchni	special
spehts•yahl•nohsh'ch' sheh•fah kooh•n'ee	
stek *stehk*	steak
stek z polędwicy *stehk spoh•lehnd•vee•tsyh*	fillet steak
strucla *stroots•lah*	strudel
suflet *soof•leht*	soufflé
surówka *soo•roof•kah*	fresh vegetable salad
surowy *soo•roh•vyh*	raw
suszone daktyle *soo•shoh•neh dahk•tyh•leh*	dried dates
suszone śliwki *soo•shoh•neh sh'leef•kee*	prunes
świeże owoce *sh'fyeh•zheh oh•voh•tseh*	fresh fruit
świeży *sh'fyeh•zhyh*	fresh
świeży daktyl *sh'fyeh•zhyh dahk•tyhl*	fresh date
syrop *syh•rohp*	syrup
szafran *shahf•rahn*	saffron
szalotka *shah•loht•kah*	shallot
szałwia *shahw•vyah*	sage

szarlotka *shahr·loht·kah*	apple pie; grass-flavored vodka with apple juice
szaszłyk *shahsh·wyhk*	lamb or mutton kebab
szczaw *shchahf*	sorrel
szczawiowa zupa *shchah·vyoh·vah zoo·pah*	sorrel soup
szczupak *shchoo·pahk*	pike
szczupak nadziewany *shchoo·pahk nah·dj'yeh·vah·nyh*	stuffed pike
szczupak w galarecie *shchoo·pahk vgah·lah·reh·ch'yeh*	pike in aspic
szczypiorek *shchyh·pyoh·rehk*	chives
szklanka *shklahn·kah*	glass
sznycel *shnyh·tsehl*	breaded pork or veal cutlet
szparag *shpah·rahg*	asparagus
szpinak *shpee·nahk*	spinach
szprotka *shproht·kah*	sprat (small herring)
sztuka mięsa *shtoo·kah myehn·sah*	portion of meat
szynka *shyhn·kah*	ham
tłusty *twoos·tyh*	fatty
tonik *toh·neek*	tonic water
tort *tohrt*	rich cake
tost *tohst*	toast
trufla *troof·lah*	truffle
truskawka *trus·kahf·kah*	strawberry
tuńczyk *toon'·chyhk*	tuna
twarożek *tfah·roh·zhehk*	fresh curd cheese
tymianek *tyh·myah·nehk*	thyme
udko *oot·koh*	leg (cut of meat)
w cieście *fch'yehsh'·ch'yeh*	in batter
w czosnku *fchohsn·koo*	in garlic
w oliwie *voh·lee·vyeh*	in olive oil

wafel _vah_•felh	waffle
wanilia vah•_n'eel_•yah	vanilla
wątróbka vohn•_troop_•kah	liver
wątróbka z kurczaka vohn•_troop_•kah skoor•_chah_•kah	chicken liver
wędlina vehn•_dlee_•nah	cold cuts
węgorz _vehn_•gohsh	eel
węgorz wędzony _vehn_•gohsh vehn•_dzoh_•nyh	smoked eel
wieprzowina vyehp•shoh•_vee_•nah	pork
winiak _vee_•n'yahk	Polish brandy
wino _vee_•noh	wine
wino deserowe _vee_•noh deh•seh•_roh_•veh	dessert wine
wino musujące _vee_•noh moo•soo•_yohn_•tseh	sparkling wine
wino stołowe _vee_•noh stoh•_woh_•veh	table wine
winogrono vee•noh•_groh_•noh	grape
winogrono czerwone vee•noh•_groh_•noh chehr•_voh_•neh	red grape
winogrono zielone vee•noh•_groh_•noh zh'yeh•_loh_•neh	white grape
wiśnia _veesh'_•n'yah	cherry
woda _voh_•dah	water
woda gazowana _voh_•dah gah•zoh•_vah_•nah	sparkling water
woda gorąca _voh_•dah goh•_rohn_•tsah	hot water
woda mineralna _voh_•dah mee•neh•_rahl_•nah	mineral water
woda niegazowana _voh_•dah n'yeh•gah•zoh•_vah_•nah	still water
woda sodowa _voh_•dah soh•_doh_•vah	soda water
woda z lodem _voh_•dah zloh•dehm	iced water
wódka _voot_•kah	vodka
wódki _voot_•kee	spirits
wół voow	ox

wołowina *voh·woh·vee·nah*	beef
z cukrem *stsoo·krehm*	with sugar
z cytryną *stsyh·tryh·nohm*	with lemon
z kością *skohsh'·ch'yohm*	on the bone
zając *zah·yohnts*	hare
zakąski *zah·kohns·kee*	appetizers
zapiekany *zah·pyeh·kah·nyh*	gratin
zboże *zboh·zheh*	grain
żeberka *zheh·behr·kah*	spare ribs
zielona fasolka *zh'yeh·loh·nah fah·sohl·kah*	green bean
zielona sałata *zh'yeh·loh·nah sah·wah·tah*	lettuce
zielony pieprz *zh'yeh·loh·nyh pyehpsh*	green pepper
ziemniak *zh'yehm·n'yahk*	potato
ziemniak pieczony *zh'yehm·n'yahk pyeh·choh·nyh*	baked potato
ziemniaki gotowane *zh'yehm·n'yah·kee goh·toh·vah·neh*	boiled potatoes
zioła mieszane *zh'yoh·wah myeh·shah·neh*	mixed herbs
zioło *zh'yoh·woh*	herb
żółtko *zhoow·tkoh*	egg yolk
żółty ser *zhoow·tyh sehr*	hard cheese
Żubrówka *zhoo·broof·kah*	grass-flavoured vodka
zupa *zoo·pah*	soup
zupa jarzynowa *zoo·pah yah·zhyh·noh·vah*	vegetable soup
zupa krem *zoo·pah krehm*	cream soup
zupa na zimno *zoo·pah nah zh'eem·noh*	cold soup
żurek (z białą kiełbasą) *zhoo·rehk (zbyah·wohm kyeh·bah·sohm)*	sour rye soup (with white sausage)

People

Conversation

ESSENTIAL

Hello	**Dzień dobry.**	dj'yehn' dohb•ryh
How are you?	**Jak się pan ma?**	yahk sh'yeh pahn mah
Fine, thanks.	**W porządku, dziękuję.**	fpoh•zhohnt•koo dz'yehn•koo•yeh
Excuse me!	**Przepraszam!**	psheh•prah•shahm
Do you speak English?	**Mówi pan po angielsku?**	moo•vee pahn poh ahn•gyehl•skoo
What's your name?	**Jak się pan nazywa?**	yahk sh'yeh pahn nah•zyh•vah
My name is…	**Nazywam się…**	nah•zyh•vahm sh'yeh…
Pleased to meet you.	**Miło mi pana poznać.**	mee•woh mee pah•nah pohz•nahch'
Where are you from?	**Skąd pan jest?**	skohnt pahn yehst
I'm from the U.S./U.K.	**Jestem z USA/Wielkiej Brytanii.**	yehs•tehm z oo•ehs•ah/vyehl•kyehy bryh•tah•n'ee
What do you do for a living?	**Czym się pan zajmuje?**	chyhm sh'yeh pahn zahy•moo•yeh
I work for…	**Pracuję w…**	prah•tsoo•yeh v…
I'm a student.	**Studiuję.**	stoo•dyoo•yeh
I'm retired.	**Jestem na emeryturze.**	yehs•tehm nah eh•meh•ryh•too•zheh
Do you like…?	**Lubi pan…?**	loo•bee pahn…
Goodbye.	**Do widzenia.**	doh vee•dzeh•n'yah
See you later.	**Do zobaczenia.**	doh zoh•bah•cheh•n'yah

Language Difficulties

Do you speak English?	**Mówi pan po angielsku?** _moo_•vee pahn po ahn•_gyehls_•koo
Does anyone here speak English?	**Czy ktoś tu zna angielski?** chyh ktohsh' too znah ahn•_gyehls_•kee
I don't speak much Polish.	**Słabo mówię po polsku.** _swah_•boh _moo_•vyeh poh _pohls_•koo
Can you speak more slowly?	**Proszę mówić wolniej.** _proh_•sheh _moo_•veech' _vohl_•n'yehy
Can you repeat that?	**Proszę powtórzyć.** _proh_•sheh pohf•_too_•zhyhch'
Excuse me? [Pardon?]	**Słucham?** _swoo_•hahm
What was that?	**Co pan powiedział?** tsoh pahn poh•_vyeh_•dj'yahw
Can you spell it?	**Może pan to przeliterować?** _moh_•zheh pahn toh psheh•leeh•teh•_roh_•vahch'
Can you write it down?	**Może pan mi to napisać?** _moh_•zheh pahn mee toh nah•_pee_•sahch'
Can you translate this into English for me?	**Może pan mi to przetłumaczyć na angielski?** _moh_•zheh pahn mee toh psheh•twoo•_mah_•chyhch' na ahn•_gyehl_•skyh
What does this mean?	**Co to znaczy?** tsoh toh _znah_•chyh
I understand.	**Rozumiem.** roh•_zoo_•myehm
I don't understand.	**Nie rozumiem.** n'yeh roh•_zoo_•myehm
Do you understand?	**Rozumie pan?** roh•_zoo_•myeh pahn

YOU MAY HEAR...

Słabo mówię po angielsku. _swah_•boh _moo_•vyeh poh ahn•_gyehls_•koo | I speak only a little English.

Nie mówię po angielsku. n'yeh _moo_•vyeh poh ahn•_gyehls_•koo | I don't speak English.

Greetings between Polish men and women have changed
during recent years. In the past men kissed women's hands as a
sign of respect. Today men and women say hello or kiss each other
on the cheek if they are good friends. In most situations you usually
say **dzień dobry**, good morning or hello. With relatives, friends and
children you can simply say **cześć**, hi.

Making Friends

Hello/Hi!	**Dzień dobry./Cześć!** *dj'yehn' dohb·ryh/chehsh'ch'*
Good morning.	**Dzień dobry.** *dj'yehn' dohb·ryh*
Good evening.	**Dobry wieczór.** *dohb·ryh vyeh·choor*
My name is...	**Nazywam się...** *nah·zyh·vahm sh'yeh...*
What's your name?	**Jak się pan nazywa?** *yahk sh'yeh pahn nah·zyh·vah*
I'd like to introduce you to...	**Chciałbym** *m* **/Chciałabym** *f* **pana przedstawić...** *hch'yahw·byhm/hch'yah·wah·byhm pah·nah psheht·stah·veech'...*
Pleased to meet you.	**Miło mi pana poznać.** *mee·woh mee pah·nah pohz·nahch'*
How are you?	**Jak się pan ma?** *yahk sh'yeh pahn mah*

| Fine, thanks. | **W porządku, dziękuję.** fpoh·<u>zhohnt</u>·koo dz'yehn·koo·yeh |
| And you? | **A pan?** ah pahn |

Travel Talk

I'm here...	**Jestem tutaj.** <u>yehs</u>·tehm <u>too</u>·tay
on business	**służbowo** <u>swoozh</u>·boh·voh
on vacation	**na wakacjach** nah vah·<u>kahts</u>·yahh
I'm studying.	**Studiuję.** stood·<u>yoo</u>·yeh
I'm staying for...	**Będę tu...** <u>beh</u>·deh too...
I've been here...	**Jestem tu...** <u>yehs</u>·tehm too...
a day	**jeden dzień** <u>yeh</u>·dehn dj'yehn'
a week	**tydzień** <u>tyh</u>·dj'yehn'
a month	**miesiąc** <u>myeh</u>·sh'yohnts
Where are you from?	**Skąd pan jest?** skohnt pahn yehst
I'm from...	**Jestem z...** <u>yehs</u>·tehm z...

For Numbers, see page 171.

For Dates, see page 174.

Personal

Who are you with?	**Z kim pan tu jest?** skeem pahn too yehst
I'm here alone.	**Jestem sam** m **/sama** f <u>yehs</u>·tehm sahm/<u>sah</u>·mah
I'm with...	**Jestem z...** <u>yehs</u>·tehm z...
my husband/wife	**moim mężem/moją żoną** <u>moh</u>·eem <u>mehn</u>·zhehm/ <u>moh</u>·yohm zhoh·nohm
my boyfriend/ girlfriend	**moim chłopakiem/moją dziewczyną** <u>moh</u>·eem <u>hwoh</u>·pah·kyehm/<u>moh</u>·yohm dj'yehf·<u>chyh</u>·nohm
a friend	**przyjacielem** m **/przyjaciółką** f pshyh·yah·<u>ch'yeh</u>·lehm/pshyh·yah·<u>ch'yoow</u>·kohm
friends	**przyjaciółmi** pshyh·yah·<u>ch'yoow</u>·myh
a colleague	**kolegą** m **/koleżanką** f **z pracy** koh·<u>leh</u>·gohm/ koh·leh·<u>zhahn</u>·kohm sprah·tsyh

colleagues	**kolegami** *m* **/koleżankami** *f* **z pracy** *koh•leh•gah•myh/koh•leh•zhahn•kah•myh sprah•tsyh*
When's your birthday?	**Kiedy ma pan urodziny?** *k'yeh•dyh mah pahn oo•roh•dj'ee•nyh*
How old are you?	**Ile ma pan lat?** *ee•leh mah pahn laht*
I'm...	**Mam...lat.** *mahm...laht*
Are you married?	**Czy jest pan żonaty** *m* **/ pani mężatką** *f* **?** *chyh yehst pahn zhoh•nah•tyh/pah•n'ee mehn•zhaht•kohm*
I'm...	**Jestem...** *yehs•tehm...*
single/ in a relationship	**wolny** *m* **/wolna** *f* **w związku** *vohl•nyh/vohl•nah/ vzvyohn•skoo*
engaged	**zaręczony** *m* **/zaręczona** *f* *zah•rehn•choh•nyh/ zah•rehn•choh•nah*
married	**żonaty** *m* **/mężatką** *f* *zhoh•nah•tyh/ mehn•zhaht•kohm*
divorced	**rozwiedziony** *m* **/rozwiedziona** *f* *rohz•vyeh•dj'yoh•nyh/rohz•vyeh•dj'yoh•nah*
separated	**w separacji** *fseh•pah•rah•tsee*
widowed	**wdowcem** *m* **/wdową** *f* *vdoh•vtsehm/vdoh•vohm*
Do you have children/ grandchildren?	**Ma pan dzieci/wnuki?** *mah pahn dj'yeh•ch'ee/ vnoo•kee*

For Numbers, see page 171.

Work & School

What do you do for a living?	**Czym się pan zajmuje?** *chyhm sh'yeh pahn zahy•moo•yeh?*
What are you studying?	**Co pan studiuje?** *tsoh pahn stood•yoo•yeh*
I'm studying...	**Studiuję...** *stood•yoo•yeh...*
I work full time/ part time.	**Pracuję na pełny etat/część etatu.** *prah•tsoo•yeh nah pehw•nyh eh•taht/chehn'sh'ch' eh•tah•too*
I'm unemployed	**Nie pracuję** *n'yeh prah•tsoo•yeh*
I work at home	**Pracuję w domu** *prah•tsoo•yeh vdoh•moo*

Who do you work for?	**Gdzie pan pracuje?** *gdj'yeh pahn prah·tsoo·yeh*
I work for…	**Pracuję w…** *prah·tsoo·yeh v…*
Here's my business card	**Oto moja wizytówka** *oh·toh moh·yah vee·zyh·toof·kah*

For Business Travel, see page 143.

Weather

What's the weather forecast?	**Jaka jest prognoza pogody?** *yah·kah yehst prohg·noh·zah poh·goh·dyh*
What beautiful/ terrible weather!	**Jaka piękna/okropna pogoda!** *yah·kah pyehnk·nah/oh·krohp·nah poh·goh·dah*
It's cool/warm.	**Jest chłodno/ciepło.** *yehst hwohd·noh/ch'yehp·wo*
It's hot/cold.	**Jest gorąco/zimno.** *yehst goh·rohn·tsoh/zh'eem·nol*
It's sunny.	**Świeci słońce.** *sh'vyeh·ch'ee swohn'·tseh*
It's rainy/snowy.	**Pada deszcz/śnieg.** *pah·dah dehshch/sh'n'yehk*
It's icy.	**Jest ślisko.** *yehst sh'lees·koh*
Do I need a jacket/ an umbrella?	**Mam wziąć kurtkę/parasol?** *mahm vzyohn'ch' koort·keh/pah·rah·sohl*

For Temperature, see page 177.

Romance

ESSENTIAL

Would you like to go out for a drink/meal?	**Może pójdziemy na drinka/coś zjeść?** *moh·zheh pooy·dj'eh·myh nah dreen·kah/tsohsh' zyehsh·ch'*
What are your plans for tonight/tomorrow?	**Masz jakieś plany na wieczór/jutro?** *mahsh yah·kyehsh' plah·nyh nah vyeh·choor/yoot·roh*
Can I have your number?	**Podasz mi swój numer telefonu?** *poh·dahsh mee sfuy noo·mehr teh·leh·foh·noo*

Can I join you?	**Mogę się dosiąść?** _moh_•geh sh'yeh _doh_•sh'yohn'sh'ch'
Can I buy you a drink?	**Mogę postawić ci drinka?** _moh_•geh pohs•_tah_•veech' ch'ee _dree_•nkah
I like/love you.	**Lubię/Kocham cię.** _loo_•bieh/_koh_•hahm ch'yeh

For Grammar, see page 166.

The Dating Game

Would you like to go out for…?	**Może pójdziemy na…?** _moh_•zheh pooy•_dj'yeh_•myh nah…
coffee	**kawę** _kah_•veh
a drink	**drinka** _dreen_•kah
dinne	**kolację** koh•_lahts_•yeh
What are your plans for…?	**Masz jakieś plany na…?** mahsh _yah_•kyehsh' _plah_•nyh nah…
today	**dzisiaj** _dj'ee_•sh'yahy
tonight	**wieczór** _vyeh_•choor
tomorrow	**jutro** _yoot_•roh
this weekend	**weekend** _wee_•kehnt

Where would you like to go?	**Dokąd chciałbyś** *m* **/chciałabyś** *f* **pójść?** *doh-kohn hch'yahw-byhsh'/hch'yah-wah-bysh' pooysh'ch'*
I'd like to go to…	**Chciałbym** *m* **/Chciałabym** *f* *pójść do…* *hch'yahw-byhm/hch'yah-wah-byhm pooysh'ch' doh…*
Do you like…?	**Lubisz…?** *loo-beesh'…?*
Can I have your number?	**Podasz mi swój numer telefonu?** *poh-dahsh mee sfooy noo-mehr teh-leh-foh-noo*
Can I have your e-mail?	**Podasz mi swój e-mail?** *poh-dahsh mee sooy ee-mehyl*
Are you on Facebook/ Twitter?	**Masz konto na Facebooku/Twitterze?** *mahsh kohn-toh nah fehys-boo-koo/twee-teh-zheh*
Can I join you?	**Mogę się dosiąść?** *moh-geh sh'yeh doh-sh'yohn'sh'ch*
Is this seat free?	**To miejsce jest wolne?** *toh myehys-tseh yehst vohl-neh*
You look great!	**Świetnie wyglądasz!** *sh'vyeht-n'yeh wyh-glohn-dahsh*
You're very attractive	**Jesteś bardzo atrakcyjny** *m* **/atrakcyjna** *f* *yehs-tehsh' bahr-dzoh ah-trahk-tsyhy-nyh/ ah-trahk-tsyhy-nah*
Let's go somewhere quieter.	**Może pójdziemy w jakieś spokojniejsze miejsce?** *moh-zheh puy-dj'yeh-myh vyah-kyehsh' spoh-kohy-n'yehy-sheh myehys-tseh*

For Communications, see page 47.

Accepting & Rejecting

I'd love to.	**Bardzo chętnie.** *bahr-dzoh chehnt-n'yeh*
Where should we meet?	**Gdzie możemy się spotkać?** *gdj'eh moh-zheh-myh sh'yeh spoht-kach'*
I'll meet you at the bar/ your hotel.	**Spotkamy się w barze/twoim hotelu.** *spoht-kah-myh sh'yeh vbah-zheh/tfoh-eem hoh-teh-loo*
I'll come by at…	**Przyjdę o…** *pshyhy-deh oh…*
What's your address?	**Gdzie mieszkasz?** *gdj'yeh myehsh-kahsh*

I'm busy.	**Jestem zajęty** m **/zajęta** f _yehs_·tehm zah·_yehn_·tyh/ zah·_yehn_·tah
I'm not interested.	**Nie jestem zainteresowany** m **/zainteresowana** f n'yeh yehs·tehm zah·een·teh·reh·soh·_vah_·nyh/ zah·een·teh·reh·soh·_vah_·nah
Leave me alone, please!	**Zostaw mnie w spokoju!** _zohs_·tahf mn'yeh fspoh·_koh_·yoo
Stop bothering me!	**Odczep się!** _oht_·chehp sh'yeh

Getting Intimate

Can I hug/kiss you?	**Mogę cię przytulić/pocałować?** _moh_·geh ch'yeh pshyh·_too_·leech'/poh·tsah·_woh_·vahch'
Yes.	**Tak.** tahk
No.	**Nie.** n'yeh
Stop!	**Przestań!** _pshehs_·tahn'
I love you	**Kocham cię** _koh_·hahm ch'yeh

Sexual Preferences

Are you gay?	**Jesteś gejem** m **/lesbijką** f? yehs·tehsh' _geh_·yehm/ lehs·_beey_·kohm
I'm…	**Jestem…** _yehs_·tehm…
heterosexual	**heteroseksualny** m **/heteroseksualna** f heh·teh·roh·sehk·soo·_ahl_·nyh/ heh·teh·roh ·sehk·soo·_ahl_·nah
gay	**gejem** m **/lesbijką** f _geh_·yehm/lehs·_beey_·kohm
bisexual	**biseksualny** m **/biseksualna** f bee·sehk·soo·_ahl_·nyh/bee·sehk·soo·_ahl_·nah
Do you like men/women?	**Wolisz mężczyzn/kobiety?** _voh_·leesh mehnzh·chyhzn/koh·_byeh_·tyh

For Grammar, see page 166

Leisure Time

Sightseeing

ESSENTIAL

Where's the tourist information office?	**Gdzie jest biuro informacji turystycznej?** *gdj'yeh yehst byoo•roh een•fohr•mah•tsyee too•ryhs•tyhch•nehy*
What are the main points of interest?	**Co tu warto zobaczyć?** *tsoh too vahr•toh zoh•bah•chyhch'*
Are there tours in English?	**Czy są wycieczki po angielsku?** *chyh sohm vyh•ch'yech•kee poh ahn•gyehl•skoo*
Can I have a map/ guide please?	**Czy mogę prosić mapę/przewodnik?** *chyh moh•geh proh•sh'eech' mah•peh/psheh•vohd•n'eek*

While visiting Poland, tourists can enjoy arts and culture throughout the year. Classical music enthusiasts should visit Chopin's birthplace, Żelazowa Wola, during the summer for free outdoor concerts. Historic Cracow features many art galleries and museums, including **Muzeum Narodowe** (National Museum) and **Muzeum Czartoryskich** (Cartoryski Museum). Warsaw, Poland's capital, is home to numerous renowned theaters and concert halls, as well as one of Europe's most beautiful city parks, **Łazienki Królewskie**. During August, the beach town of Sopot entertains music lovers with its International Pop Festival.

Tourist Information

Do you have any information on...?	**Czy ma pan jakieś informacje o...?** *chyh mah pahn yah•kyehsh' een•fohr•mah•tsyeh oh...*
Can you recommend...?	**Czy może pan polecić...?** *chyh moh•zheh pahn poh•leh•ch'eech'...*

a bus tour	**wycieczkę autobusową** *vyh·ch'yehch·keh ahw·toh·boo·soh·wohm*
a boat trip	**rejs statkiem** *rehys staht·kyehm*
an excursion	**wycieczkę** *vyh·ch'yehch·keh*
a sightseeing tour	**wycieczkę po mieście** *vyh·ch'yehch·keh poh myehsh'·ch'yeh*

Most cities and large towns have a tourist information office. They are usually located in the center of town; some display the sign **IT** (**informacja turystyczna**). Tourist information can also be obtained from **Orbis** and **PTTK** (Polish Tourist Organization) offices. Most bookstores and tourist offices sell road, regional and local maps. Town maps are displayed on kiosks in major squares and streets and at tourist information offices.

On Tour

I'd like to go on the excursion to…	**Interesuje mnie wycieczka do…** *een·teh·reh·soo·yeh mn'yeh vyh·ch'yehch·kah doh…*
When's the next tour?	**Kiedy będzie następna wycieczka?** *kyeh·dyh behn·dj'yeh nahs·tehmp·nah vyh·ch'yech·kah*
Are there tours in English?	**Czy są wycieczki po angielsku?** *chyh sohm vyh·ch'yech·kee poh ahn·gyehl·skoo*
Is there an English guide book/audio guide?	**Czy jest przewodnik/audioprzewodnik w języku angielskim?** *chyh yehst pshe·vohd·n'eek/ahwdyoh·pshe·vohd·n'eek vyehn·zyh·koo ahn·gyehl·skyhm*
What time do we leave/return?	**O której wyruszamy/wracamy?** *oh ktoo·rehy vyh·roo·shah·myh/vrah·tsah·myh*
We'd like to see the…	**Chcielibyśmy zobaczyć…** *hch'yeh·lee·byhsh'·myh zoh·bah·chyhch'…*

Can we stop here...?	**Czy możemy się tu zatrzymać...?** *chyh moh‑zheh‑myh sh'yeh too zaht‑shyh‑mahch'...*
to take photos	**żeby zrobić zdjęcia** *zheh‑byh zroh‑beech' zdyehn‑ch'yah*
to buy souvenirs	**żeby kupić pamiątki** *zheh‑byh koo‑peech' pah‑myohnt‑kee*
to use the restrooms [toilets]	**żeby skorzystać z toalety** *zheh‑byh skoh‑zhyhs‑tahch' stoh‑ah‑leh‑tyh*
Is it disabled-accessible?	**Czy jest dostęp dla niepełnosprawnych?** *chyh yehst dohs‑tehmp dlah n'yeh‑pehw‑noh‑sprahv‑nyhh*

For Tickets, see page 19.

Seeing the Sights

Where's...?	**Gdzie jest/są...?** *gdj'yeh yehst/sohm*
the battleground	**pole bitwy** *poh‑leh beet‑fyh*
the botanical garden	**ogród botaniczny** *oh‑groot boh‑tah‑n'eech‑nyh*
the castle	**zamek** *zah‑mehk*
the cathedral	**katedra** *kah‑teh‑drah*
the church	**kościół** *kosh'‑ch'yoow*
the downtown area	**centrum** *tsehn‑troom*
the fountain	**fontanna** *fohn‑tahn‑nah*
the library	**biblioteka** *beeb‑lyoh‑teh‑kah*
the market	**bazar** *bah‑zahr*
the monument	**pomnik** *pohm‑n'eek*
the museum	**muzeum** *moo‑zeh‑oom*
the old town	**stare miasto** *stah‑reh myahs‑toh*
the opera house	**opera** *oh‑peh‑rah*
the palace	**pałac** *pah‑wahts*
the park	**park** *pahrk*
the ruins	**ruiny** *roo‑ee‑nyh*
the shopping area	**centrum handlowe** *tsehn‑troom hahn‑dloh‑veh*

the town square	**rynek** _ryh_·nehk
the town hall	**ratusz** _rah_·toosh
Can you show me on the map?	**Czy może mi pan pokazać na mapie?** _chyh_ _moh_·zheh mee pahn poh·_kah_·zahch' nah _mah_·pyeh
It's…	**To jest…** toh yehst…
amazing	**niesamowite** n'yeh·sah·moh·_vee_·teh
beautiful	**piękne** _pyehnk_·neh
boring	**nudne** _nood_·neh
interesting	**interesujące** een·teh·reh·soo·_yohn_·tseh
magnificent	**wspaniałe** vspah·_n'yah_·weh
romantic	**romantyczne** roh·mahn·_tyhch_·neh
strange	**dziwne** _dj'eev_·neh
stunning	**olśniewające** ohl·sh'n'yeh·vah·_yohn_·tseh
terrible	**okropne** ohk·_rohp_·neh
ugly	**brzydkie** _bzhyht_·kyeh
I (don't) like it.	**(Nie) Podoba mi się to.** (n'yeh) poh·_doh_·bah mee sh'yeh toh

For Asking Directions, see page 34.

Religious Sites

Where's…?	**Gdzie jest…?** gdj'yeh yehst
the cathedral	**katedra** kah·_teh_·drah
the Catholic/ Protestant church	**kościół katolicki/protestancki** _kosh'_·ch'yoow kah·toh·_lee_·tskee/ proh·tehs·_tahn_·tskee
the mosque	**meczet** _meh_·cheht
the shrine	**kapliczka** kah·_pleech_·kah
the synagogue	**synagoga** syh·nah·_goh_·gah
What time is mass/ the service?	**O której jest msza/nabożeństwo?** oh _ktoo_·rehy yehst mshah/nah·boh·_zhehn'_·stfoh

Shopping

ESSENTIAL

Where is the market/ mall [shopping centre]?	**Gdzie jest targ/centrum handlowe?** *gdj'yeh yehst tahrk/tsehn·troom hahn·dloh·veh*
I'm just browsing.	**Tylko się rozglądam.** *tyhl·koh sh'yeh rohz·glohn·dahm*
Can you help me?	**Czy może mi pan pomóc?** *chyh moh·zheh mee pahn poh·moots*
I'm being helped.	**Jestem już obsługiwany m /obsługiwana f.** *yehs·tehm yoosh ohp·swoo·gee·vah·nyh/ ohp·swoo·gee·vah·nah*
How much is this/that?	**Ile to/tamto kosztuje?** *ee·leh toh/tahm·toh kosh·too·yeh*
Can you show me…?	**Może mi pan pokazać…?** *moh·zheh mee pahn poh·kah·zahch'…*
This/That one, please.	**Proszę to/tamto.** *proh·sheh toh/tahm·toh*
That's all, thanks.	**To wszystko, dziękuję.** *toh fshyhs·tkoh dj'yehn·koo·yeh*

Where can I pay?	**Gdzie mogę zapłacić?** *gdj'yeh moh‧geh zah‧pwah‧ch'eech'*
I'll pay in cash/ by credit card.	**Zapłacę gotówką/kartą kredytową.** *zah‧pwah‧tseh goh‧toof‧kohm/kahr‧tohm kreh‧dyh‧toh‧vohm*
A receipt, please.	**Proszę paragon.** *proh‧sheh pah‧rah‧gohn*

At the Shops

Where is/are…?	**Gdzie jest/są…?** *gdj'yeh yehst/sohm…*
When does…open/ close?	**Od/Do której czynny jest…?** *ohd/doh ktoo‧rehy chyhn‧nyh yehst…*
the antiques store	**antykwariat** *ahn‧tyh‧kfah‧ryaht*
the bakery	**piekarnia** *pyeh‧kahr‧n'yah*
the bank	**bank** *bahnk*
the butcher shop	**sklep mięsny** *sklehp myehn‧snyh*
the bookstore	**księgarnia** *ksh'yehn‧gahr‧n'yah*
the camera shop	**sklep fotograficzny** *sklehp foh‧toh‧grah‧feech‧nyh*
the clothing store	**sklep odzieżowy** *sklehp oh‧dj'yeh‧zhoh‧vyh*
the delicatessen	**delikatesy** *deh‧lee‧kah‧teh‧syh*
the department store	**dom towarowy** *dohm toh‧vah‧roh‧vyh*
the florist	**kwiaciarnia** *kfyah‧ch'yahr‧n'yah*
the gift shop	**sklep z upominkami** *sklehp zoo‧poh‧meen‧kah‧mee*
grocery store	**sklep spożywczy** *sklehp spoh‧zhyhf‧chyh*
the health food store	**sklep ze zdrową żywnością** *sklehp zeh zdroh‧vohm zhyhv‧nohsh'‧ch'yohm*
the jeweler	**jubiler** *yoo‧bee‧lehr*
the liquor store [off-licence]	**sklep monopolowy** *sklehp moh‧noh‧poh‧loh‧vyh*
market	**bazar** *bah‧zahr*
the music store	**sklep muzyczny** *sklehp moo‧zyhch‧nyh*

the pastry shop	**cukiernia** *tsoo-kyehr-n'yah*
the pharmacy [chemist]	**apteka** *ahp-teh-kah*
the produce [grocery] store	**sklep z artykułami spożywczymi** *sklehp zahr-tyh-koo-wah-mee spoh-zhyhf-chyh-mee*
the shoe store	**sklep obuwniczy** *sklehp oh-boov-n'ee-chyh*
the shopping mall [centre]	**centrum handlowe** *tsehn-troom hahn-dloh-veh*
the souvenir store	**sklep z pamiątkami** *sklehp spahm-yohnt-kah-mee*
the sporting store	**sklep sportowy** *sklehp spohr-toh-vyh*
the supermarket	**supermarket** *soo-pehr-mahr-keht*
the tobacconist	**sklep tytoniowy** *sklehp tyh-toh-n'yoh-vyh*
the newsstand	**kiosk z gazetami** *kyohsk zgah-zeh-tah-mee*
the toy store	**sklep z zabawkami** *sklehp zzah-bahf-kah-mee*

Ask an Assistant

What are the opening hours?	**Jakie są godziny otwarcia?** *yah-kyeh sohm goh-dj'ee-nyh oht-fahr-ch'yah*
Where is/are…?	**Gdzie jest/są…?** *gdj'yeh yehst/sohm…*
the cashier	**kasa** *kah-sah*
the escalators	**schody ruchome** *shoh-dyh roo-hoh-meh*
the elevator [lift]	**winda** *veen-dah*

the fitting room	**przymierzalnia** pshyh·myeh·<u>zhahl</u>·n'yah
the store directory [guide]	**tablica informacyjna** tah·<u>blee</u>·tsah een·fohr·mah·<u>tsyhy</u>·nah
Can you help me?	**Czy może mi pan pomóc?** chyh <u>moh</u>·zheh mee pah poh·moots
I'm just looking	**Tylko się rozglądam** tyhl·koh sh'yeh rohz·<u>glohn</u>·dahm
I'm being helped.	**Jestem już obsługiwany** m/**obsługiwana**f. yehs·tehm yoosh ohp·swoo·gee·<u>vah</u>·nyh/ ohp·swoo·gee·<u>vah</u>·nah
Do you have…?	**Czy mają państwo…?** chyh <u>mah</u>·yohm pahn'·stfoh..
Can you show me…?	**Czy może mi pan pokazać…?** chyh <u>moh</u>·zheh mee pahn poh·<u>kah</u>·zahch'…
Can you ship/wrap it?	**Można prosić o wysłanie/opakowanie?** <u>mohzh</u>·na proh·sh'eech' oh vyh·<u>swah</u>·n'yeh/oh·pah·koh·<u>vah</u>·n'yeh
How much?	**Ile to kosztuje?** <u>ee</u>·leh toh kohsh·<u>too</u>·yeh
That's all, thanks.	**To wszystko, dziękuję.** toh <u>fshyhst</u>·koh dj'yehn·<u>koo</u>·yeh

For Clothing, see page 124.
For Meals & Cooking, see page 65.
For Souvenirs, see page 130.

YOU MAY HEAR…

Czym mogę służyć? chyhm <u>moh</u>·geh <u>swoo</u>·zhyhch'	Can I help you?
Chwileczkę. hvee·<u>lehch</u>·keh	One moment.
Co podać? tsoh poh·dahch'	What would you like?
To wszystko? toh <u>fshyhst</u>·koh	Is that all?

YOU MAY SEE...

Zamknięte/otwarte	open/closed
Przerwa śniadaniowa	closed for lunch
Przymierzalnia	fitting room
Kasa	cashier
Płatność tylko gotówką	cash only
Przyjmujemy karty kredytowe	credit cards accepted
Godziny otwarcia	business hours
Wyjście	exit

Personal Preferences

I want something...	**Chciałbym** m **/Chciałabym** f **coś...** *hch'yahw•byhm/hch'yah•wah•byhm tsohsh'...*
cheap/expensive	**taniego/drogiego** *tah•n'yeh•goh/droh•gyeh•goh*
larger/smaller	**większego/mniejszego** *vyehn•ksheh•goh/ mn'yehy•sheh•goh*
from this region	**miejscowego** *myehy•stsoh•veh•goh*
Around...euros/złotych.	**około ... euro** *oh•koh•woh ... ehw•roh/zwoh•tyhh*
Is it real/fake?	**Czy to jest prawdziwe/sztuczne?** *chyh toh yehst prahv•dj'ee•veh/shtoo•chneh*
Could I see this/that?	**Czy mogę zobaczyć to/tamto?** *chyh moh•geh zoh•bah•chyhch' toh/tahm•toh*
That's not quite what I want.	**To nie to, czego szukam.** *toh n'yeh toh cheh•goh shoo•kahm*
I don't like it.	**To mi się nie podoba.** *toh mee sh'yeh n'yeh poh•doh•bah*
It's too expensive	**To jest za drogie** *toh yehst zah droh•gyeh*
I'd like to think about it.	**Chcę się nad tym zastanowić.** *htseh sh'yeh naht tyhm zahs•tah•noh•veech'*
I'll take it.	**Wezmę to.** *vehz•meh toh*

Paying & Bargaining

How much?	**Ile to kosztuje?** *ee•leh toh kosh•too•yeh*
I'll pay in cash/ by credit card/ by traveler's check.	**Zapłacę gotówką/kartą kredytową/czekiem podróżnym.** *zah•pwah•tseh goh•toof•kohm/ kahr•tohm kreh•dyh•toh•vohm/cheh•kyehm pohd•roozh•nyhm*
A receipt, please.	**Proszę paragon.** *proh•sheh pah•rah•gohn*
That's too much.	**To za drogo.** *toh zah droh•goh*
I'll give you…	**Dam panu…** *dahm pah•noo…*
I only have…zlotys.	**Mam tylko…złotych.** *mahm tyhl•koh…zwoh•tyhh*
Is that your best price?	**To najniższa cena?** *toh nay•n'eezh•shah tseh•nah*
Can you give me a discount?	**Da mi pan zniżkę?** *dah mee pahn zn'eezh•keh*

For Numbers, see page 171.

YOU MAY HEAR…

Jak chce pan zapłacić? *yahk htseh pahn zah•pwah•ch'eech'*	How are you paying?
Transakcja została odrzucona. *trahn•sahk•tsyah zoh•stah•wah ohd•zhoo•tsoh•nah*	Your credit card has been declined.
Proszę o dowód tożsamości. *proh•sheh oh doh•voot tohzh•sah•moh•sh'ch'ee*	ID, please.
Nie przyjmujemy kart kredytowych. *n'yeh pshyh•ymoo•yeh•myh kahrt kreh•dyh•toh•vyhh*	We don't accept credit cards.
Płatność tylko gotówką. *pwaht•nohsh'ch' tyhl•koh goh•toof•kohm*	Cash only, please.

Cash is the preferred method of paying in stores. Larger stores
and retail chains usually accept major credit cards. Travelers
checks and personal checks are rarely accepted in Poland.

Making a Complaint

I'd like...	**Chciałbym** *m* **/Chciałabym** *f*... *hch'yahw•byhm/ hch'yah•wah•byhm...*
to exchange this	**to wymienić** *toh vyh•myeh•n'eech'*
to return this	**to oddać** *toh ohd•dahch'*
a refund	**zwrot pieniędzy** *zvroht pyeh•n'ehn•dzyh*
to see the manager	**porozmawiać z kierownikiem** *poh•rohz•mah•vyahch' skyeh•rohv•n'ee•kyehm*
Here's the receipt.	**Oto paragon.** *oh•toh pah•rah•gohn*

Services

Can you recommend...?	**Czy może pan polecić...?** *chyh moh•zheh pahn poh•leh•ch'eech'...*
a barber	**fryzjera męskiego** *fryh•zyeh•rah mehn•skyeh•goh*
a dry cleaner	**pralnię chemiczną** *prahl•n'yeh heh•meech•nohm*
a hairdresser	**fryzjera** *fryh•zyeh•rah*
a laundromat [launderette]	**pralnię samoobsługową** *prahl•n'yeh sah•moh•ohp•swoo•goh•vohm*
a nail salon	**manikiurzystkę** *mah•nee•kyoo•zhyhs•tkeh*
a spa	**spa** *spah*
a travel agency	**biuro podróży** *byoo•roh pohd•roo•zhyh*
Can you...this?	**Może pan to...?** *moh•zheh pahn toh...*
alter	**poprawić** *poh•prah•veech'*
clean	**wyczyścić** *vyh•chyhsh'•ch'eech'*
mend	**załatać** *zah•wah•tahch'*
press	**wyprasować** *vyh•prah•soh•vahch'*

| When will it be ready? | **Na kiedy to będzie gotowe?** *nah <u>kyeh</u>•dyh toh <u>behn</u>•dj'yeh goh•<u>toh</u>•veh* |

Hair & Beauty

I'd like an appointment for today/tomorrow.	**Chciałbym** *m* **/Chciałabym** *f* **umówić się na dzisiaj/ jutro.** *<u>hch'yahw</u>•byhm /<u>hch'yah</u>•wah•byhm oo•<u>moo</u>•veech sh'yeh nah <u>dj'ee</u>•sh'yahy/<u>yoot</u>•roh*
I'd like…	**Poproszę o…** *poh•<u>proh</u>•sheh oh…*
some colour/ highlights	**trochę koloru/pasemka** *<u>troh</u>•heh koh•<u>loh</u>•roo/ pah•<u>sehm</u>•kah*
my hair styled/ blow-dried	**ułożenie/wysuszenie włosów** *oo•woh•<u>zheh</u>•n'yeh/ vyh•soo•<u>sheh</u>•n'yeh <u>vwoh</u>•soof*
a haircut	**strzyżenie** *st•shyh•<u>zheh</u>•n'yeh*
an eyebrow/ bikini wax	**depilację brwi/bikini woskiem** *deh•pee•<u>lahts</u>•yeh brvee/bee•<u>kee</u>•n'ee <u>vohs</u>•kyehm*
a facial	**zabieg na twarz** *<u>zah</u>•byehk nah <u>tfahsh</u>*
a manicure/pedicure	**manicure/pedicure** *<u>mah</u>•n'ee•kyoor/<u>peh</u>•dee•kyoor*
a (sports) massage	**masaż (sportowy)** *<u>mah</u>•sash (spohr•<u>toh</u>•vyh)*
a trim	**podcięcie włosów** *poht•<u>ch'yen</u>•ch'yeh <u>vwoh</u>•soof*
Not too short	**Nie za krótko** *n'yeh zah <u>kroot</u>•koh*
Shorter here	**Krócej tutaj** *<u>kroot</u>•tsehy <u>too</u>•tahy*

Do you offer...?	**Czy prowadzą państwo...?** *chyh proh·vah·dzohm*
	pahn's·tfoh...
I'd like...	**Poproszę o...** *poh·proh·sheh oh...*
acupuncture	**akupunkturę** *ah·koo·poon·ktoo·reh*
aromatherapy	**aromaterapię** *ah·roh·mah·teh·rah·pyeh*
oxygen treatment	**terapię tlenową** *teh·rah·pyeh tleh·noh·vohm*
Is there a sauna?	**Czy jest sauna?** *chyh yehst sahw·nah*

Throughout Poland, there are many popular health resorts
of long-standing tradition (Busko-Zdrój, Konstancin Jeziorna,
Duszniki Zdrój, Krynica, Nałęczów, Szczawnica) where the waters
are known to have healing qualities. Spas and wellness centers, day
and overnight, can be found in large cities and seaside resorts (Jurata,
Jastarnia, Łeba, Sopot, Ustka), the lake region (Augustów) and the
mountains (Zakopane, Bielsko-Biała). These offer a wide range of high-
quality services and are usually relatively expensive.

Antiques

How old is this?	**Ile to ma lat?** *ee·leh toh mah laht*
Do you have anything from the...period?	**Ma pan coś z okresu...?** *mah pahn tsohsh' zoh·kreh·soo...*
Do I have to fill out any forms?	**Czy muszę wypełniać jakiś formularz?** *chyh moo·sheh vyh·pehw·n'yahch' yah·keesh' fohr·moo·lahsh*
Is there a certificate of authenticity?	**Czy to ma świadectwo autentyczności?** *chyh toh mah sh'fyah·dehts·tfoh aw·tehn·tyhch·nohsh'·ch'ee*
Can you ship/wrap it?	**Można prosić o wysłanie/opakowanie tego?** *mohzh·nah proh·sh'eech' oh vyh·swah·n'yeh/ oh·pah·koh·vah·n'yeh teh·goh*

Clothing

I'd like…	**Chciałbym** *m* **/Chciałabym** *f*… *hch'yahw•byhm/* *hch'yah•wah•byhm*…
Can I try this on?	**Czy mogę to przymierzyć?** *chyh moh•geh toh pshyh•myeh•zhyhch'*
It doesn't fit.	**To nie pasuje.** *toh n'yeh pah•soo•yeh*
It's too…	**To jest za…** *toh yehst zah…*
big	**duże** *doo•zheh*
small	**małe** *mah•weh*
short	**krótkie** *kroot•kyeh*
long	**długie** *dwoo•gyeh*
tight	**ciasne** *ch'yah•sneh*
loose	**luźne** *loo•zh'neh*
Do you have this in size…?	**Czy jest rozmiar…?** *chyh yehst rohz•myahr…*
Do you have this in a bigger/smaller size?	**Czy są większe/mniejsze rozmiary?** *chyh sohm vyehnk•sheh/mn'yehy•sheh rohz•myah•ryh*

For Numbers, see page 171.

For Clothes & Accessories, see page 126.

YOU MAY HEAR...

Świetnie w tym pan wygląda *sh'vyeht•n'yeh*   That looks great on you.
pahn ftyhm wyh•glohn•dah

Jak to pasuje? *yahk toh pah•soo•yeh*   How does it fit?

Nie mamy pana rozmiaru *n'yeh mah•myh*   We don't have your size.
pah•nah rohz•myah•roo

YOU MAY SEE...

ODZIEŻ DAMSKA	men's clothing
ODZIEŻ MĘSKA	women's clothing
UBRANIA DLA DZIECI	children's clothing

Colors

I want something...	**Chciałbym** *m* /**Chciałabym** *f* **coś w kolorze...**	
	hch'yahw•byhm /*hch'yah•wah•byhm tsohsh'*	
	fkoh•loh•zheh...	
beige	**beżowym**	*beh•zhoh•vyhm*
black	**czarnym**	*chahr•nyhm*
blue	**niebieskim**	*n'yeh•byehs•keem*
brown	**brązowym**	*brohn•zoh•vyhm*
gray	**szarym**	*shah•ryhm*
green	**zielonym**	*zh'yeh•loh•nyhm*
olive	**oliwkowym**	*oh•leef•koh•vyhm*
orange	**pomarańczowym**	*poh•mah•rahn'•choh•vyhm*
pink	**różowym**	*roo•zhoh•vyhm*
purple	**fioletowym**	*fioh•leh•toh•vyhm*
red	**czerwonym**	*chehr•voh•nyhm*

| white | **białym** _byah_•wyhm |
| yellow | **żółtym** _zhoow_•tyhm |

Clothes & Accessories

a backpack	**plecak** _pleh_•tsahk
a bag	**torba** _tohr_•bah
a belt	**pasek** _pah_•sehk
a bikini	**bikini** bee•_kee_•n'ee
a blouse	**bluzka** _bloos_•kah
a bra	**biustonosz** byoos•_toh_•nohsh
briefs [underpants]/	**majtki (for both sexes)/slipy (for men)/**
panties	**figi (for women)** _mahyt_•kee/ _slee_•pyh/ _fee_•gee
a coat (long/short)	**płaszcz/kurtka** pwahshch/_koort_•kah
a dress	**sukienka** soo•_kyehn_•kah
a hat	**kapelusz** kah•_peh_•loosh
a jacket	**marynarka** _m_ /**żakiet** _f_ mah•ryh•_nahr_•kah/
	zhah•kyeht
jeans	**dżinsy** _dj'een_•syh
pajamas	**piżama** pee•_zhah_•mah
pants [trousers]	**spodnie** _spohd_•n'yeh
pantyhose [tights]	**rajstopy** ray•_stoh_•pyh
a purse [handbag]	**torebka** toh•_rehp_•kah
a raincoat	**płaszcz przeciwdeszczowy** pwahshch
	psheh•ch'eev•dehsh•_choh_•vyh
a scarf	**szalik** _shah_•leek
a shirt	**koszula** _m_ /**bluzka** _f_ koh•_shoo_•lah /_bloos_•kah
shorts	**szorty** _shohr_•tyh
a skirt	**spódnica** spood•_n'ee_•tsah
socks	**skarpetki** skahr•_peht_•kee
stockings	**pończochy** pohn'•_choh_•hyh
a suit	**garnitur** _m_ /**kostium** _f_ gahr•_n'ee_•toor /_kohs_•tyoom

sunglasses	**okulary przeciwsłoneczne** *oh-koo-lah-ryh psheh-ch'eef-swoh-nehch-neh*
a sweater	**sweter** *sfeh-tehr*
a sweatshirt	**bluza** *bloo-zah*
swimming trunks	**kąpielówki** *kohm-pyeh-loof-kee*
a swimsuit	**kostium kąpielowy** *kohs-tyoom kohm-pyeh-loh-vyh*
a T-shirt	**t-shirt** *tee-shehrt*
a tie	**krawat** *krah-vaht*
underwear	**bielizna** *byeh-lee-znah*

Fabric

I'd like…	**Chciałbym** *m* **/Chciałabym** *f* **coś…** *hch'yahw-byhm /hch'yah-wah-byhm tsohsh'…*
cotton	**z bawełny** *zbah-vehw-nyh*
denim	**z dżinsu** *zdjeen-soo*
lace	**z koronki** *skoh-rohn-kee*
leather	**ze skóry** *zeh skoo-ryh*
linen	**z lnu** *zlnoo*
silk	**z jedwabiu** *zyehd-vah-byoo*
wool	**z wełny** *zvehw-nyh*
Is it machine washable?	**Czy można to prać w pralce?** *chyh mohzh-nah toh prahch' fprahl-tseh*

Shoes

I'd like…	**Chciałbym** *m* **/Chciałabym** *f*… *hch'yahw-byhm / hch'yah-wah-byhm…*
high-heeled/ flat shoes	**buty na wysokim obcasie/płaskim obcasie** *boo-tyh nah vyh-soh-keem ohp-tsah-sh'yeh/ pwahs-keem ohp-tsah-sh'yeh*
boots	**botki** *boht-kee*
loafers	**mokasyny** *moh-kah-syh-nyh*
sandals	**sandały** *sahn-dah-wyh*

shoes	**buty** _boo·tyh_
slippers	**kapcie** _kahp·ch'yeh_
sneakers	**buty sportowe** _boo·tyh spohr·toh·veh_
In size…	**Rozmiar…** _rohz·myahr…_

For Numbers, see page 171.

Sizes

small (S)	**mały/S** _mah·wyh/ehs_
medium (M)	**średni/M** _sh'rehd·n'ee/ehm_
large (L)	**duży/L** _doo·zhyh/ehl_
extra large (XL)	**bardzo duży/XL** _bahr·dzoh doo·zhyh/eeks·ehl_
petite	**rozmiar petite** _rohz·myahr peh·teet_
plus size	**rozmiar plus** _rohz·myahr ploos_

Newsagent & Tobacconist

Do you sell English-language newspapers?	**Czy sprzedają państwo gazety anglojęzyczne?** _chyh spsheh·dah·yohm pahn'·stfoh gah·zeh·tyh anh·gloh·yehn·zyhch·neh_
I'd like…	**Poproszę…** _poh·proh·sheh…_
candy	**cukierka/batonik** _coo·kyehr·kah/bah·toh·n'eek_
chewing gum	**gumę do żucia** _goo·meh doh zhoo·ch'yah_
a chocolate bar	**tabliczkę czekolady** _tahb·leech·keh cheh·koh·lah·dy_
a cigar	**cygaro** _tsyh·gah·roh_
a pack/carton of cigarettes	**paczkę/karton papierosów** _pahch·keh/kahr·tohn pah·pyeh·roh·soof_
a lighter	**zapalniczkę** _zah·pahl·n'eech·keh_
a magazine	**pismo** _pees·moh_
matches	**zapałki** _zah·pahw·kee_
a newspaper	**gazetę** _gah·zeh·the_
a pen	**długopis** _dwoo·goh·pees_
a postcard	**pocztówkę** _pohcz·toof·keh_

a road/town map...	**mapę drogową/miasta...** *mah·peh droh·goh·vohm/myah·stah...*
stamps	**znaczki** *znahch·kee*

Photography

I'm looking for...	**Szukam...aparatu fotograficznego.** *shoo·kahm... ah·pah·rah·too foh·toh·grah·feech·neh·goh*
camera.	
an automatic	**automatycznego** *ahw·toh·mah·tyhch·neh·goh*
a digital	**cyfrowego** *tsyhf·roh·veh·goh*
a disposable	**jednorazowego** *yehd·noh·rah·zoh·veh·goh*
I'd like...	**Poproszę...** *poh·proh·sheh...*
a battery	**baterię** *bah·teh·ryeh*
digital prints	**wydruki zdjęć z aparatu cyfrowego** *vyh·droo·kee zdyehnch' zah·pah·rah·too tsyhf·roh·veh·goh*
a memory card	**kartę pamięci** *kahr·teh pah·myehn'·ch'ee*
Can I print digital photos here?	**Czy mogę tu wydrukować zdjęcia z aparatu cyfrowego?** *chyh moh·geh too vyh·droo·koh·vach' zdyehn'·ch'yah zah·pah·rah·too tsyhf·roh·veh·goh*
When will the photos be ready?	**Na kiedy zdjęcia będą gotowe?** *nah kyeh·dyh zdyehn'·ch'yah behn·dohm goh·toh·veh*

Souvenirs

amber jewelry	**biżuteria z bursztynu** *bee·zhoo·<u>teh</u>·ryah zboor·<u>shtyh</u>·noo*
box of chocolates	**pudełko czekoladek/bombonierka** *poo·<u>dehw</u>·ko cheh·koh·<u>lah</u>·dehk/bohm·boh·<u>n'yehr</u>·kah*
crystal	**kryształ** *<u>kryhsh</u>·tahw*
cut glass	**szlifowane szkło** *shlee·foh·<u>vah</u>·neh shkwoh*
hand-painted eggs	**pisanki** *pee·<u>sahn</u>·kee*
hand-painted wooden box	**ręcznie malowane drewniane pudełko** *<u>rehnch</u>·n'yeh mah·loh·<u>vah</u>·neh drehv·<u>n'yah</u>·neh poo·<u>dehw</u>·koh*
key ring	**breloczek na klucze** *breh·<u>loh</u>·chehk nah <u>kloo</u>·cheh*
Polish vodka	**polska wódka** *<u>pohl</u>·skah <u>voot</u>·kah*
postcard	**pocztówka** *pohch·<u>toof</u>·kah*
poster	**plakat** *<u>plah</u>·kaht*
silver jewelry	**biżuteria ze srebra** *bee·zhoo·<u>teh</u>·ryah zeh <u>sreh</u>·brah*
tapestry	**kilim** *<u>kee</u>·leem*
T-shirt	**t-shirt** *<u>tee</u>·shehrt*
wood carving	**figurka z drewna** *fee·<u>goor</u>·kah <u>zdrehv</u>·nah*
Could I see this/that?	**Czy mogę zobaczyć to/tamto?** *chyh <u>moh</u>·geh zoh·<u>bah</u>·chyhch' toh/<u>tahm</u>·toh*

It's the one in the window/display case.	**To ten na wystawie/w gablocie.** *toh tehn nah vyhs·tah·vyeh/vgah·bloh·ch'yeh*
I'd like…	**Chciałbym** *m* **/Chciałabym** *f***…** *hch'yahw·byhm/ hch'yah·wah·byhm…*
a battery	**baterię** *bah·teh·ryeh*
a bracelet	**bransoletkę** *brahn·soh·leht·keh*
a brooch	**broszkę** *brohsh·keh*
earrings	**kolczyki** *kohl·chyh·kee*
a necklace	**naszyjnik** *nah·shyhy·n'eek*
a ring	**pierścionek** *pyehr·sh'ch'yoh·nehk*
a watch	**zegarek** *zeh·gah·rehk*
I'd like…	**Chciałbym** *m* **/Chciałabym** *f* **coś…** *hch'yahw·byhm /hch'yah·wah·byhm tsohsh'…*
amber	**z bursztynu** *zboor·shtyh·noo*
copper	**z miedzi** *zmyeh·dj'ee*
crystal (quartz)	**z kryształu** *zkryhsh·tah·woo*
diamond	**z brylantami** *zbryh·lahn·tah·mee*
enamel	**z emalii** *zeh·mah·lee*
white/yellow gold	**z białego/żółtego złota** *z byah·weh·goh/ zhoow·teh·goh zwoh·tah*
pearl	**z pereł** *speh·rehw*
pewter	**z cyny** *s·tsyh·nyh*
platinum	**z platyny** *splah·tyh·nyh*
silver	**ze srebra** *zeh sreh·brah*
stainless steel	**ze stali nierdzewnej** *zeh stah·lee n'yeh·rdzehv·nehy*
Is this real?	**Czy to jest prawdziwe?** *chyh toh yehst prahv·dj'ee·veh*
Can you engrave it?	**Można na tym grawerować?** *moh·zhnah nah tyhm grah·veh·roh·vach'*

Sport & Leisure

ESSENTIAL

Where's the game?	**Gdzie grają?** _gdj'yeh <u>grah</u>•yohm_
Where's...?	**Gdzie jest...?** _gdj'yeh yehst..._
the beach	**plaża** _<u>plah</u>•zhah_
the park	**park** _pahrk_
the pool	**basen** _<u>bah</u>•sehn_
Is it safe to swim/ dive here?	**Można tu bezpiecznie pływać/skakać?** _<u>mohzh</u>•nah too behs•<u>pyehch</u>•n'yeh <u>pwyh</u>•vahch'/<u>skah</u>•kahch'_
I'd like to rent [hire] golf clubs.	**Chciałbym** _m_ **/Chciałabym** _f_ **wypożyczyć kije golfowe.** _hch'yahw•byhm/hch'yah•wah•byhm fvyh•poh•<u>zhyh</u>•chyhch' <u>kee</u>•yeh gohl•<u>foh</u>•veh_
What's the charge per hour?	**Jaka jest opłata za godzinę?** _<u>yah</u>•kah yehst oh•<u>pwah</u>•tah zah goh•<u>dj'ee</u>•neh_
How far is it to...from here?	**Jak daleko jest stąd do...?** _yahk dah•<u>leh</u>•koh yehst stohnt doh..._
Can you show me on the map?	**Czy może mi pan pokazać na mapie?** _chyh <u>moh</u>•zheh mee pahn poh•<u>kah</u>•zahch' nah <u>mah</u>•pyeh_

Watching Sport

When is...?	**Kiedy jest/są...?** _kyeh·dyh yehst/sohm..._
the basketball game	**mecz koszykówki** _mehch koh·shyh·koof·kee_
the boxing match	**zawody bokserskie** _zah·voh·dyh bohk·sehr·skyeh_
the cycling race	**wyścig rowerowy** _vyhsh'·ch'eeg roh·veh·roh·vyh_
the golf tournament	**zawody golfowe** _zah·voh·dyh gohl·foh·veh_
the soccer [football] game	**mecz piłki nożnej** _mehch peew·kee nohzh·nehy_
the tennis match	**mecz tenisowy** _mehch teh·n'ee·soh·vyh_
Who's playing?	**Kto gra?** _ktoh grah_
Where's...?	**Gdzie jest...?** _gdj'yeh yehst..._
the horsetrack	**tor wyścigów konnych** _tohr vyhsh'·ch'ee·goof kohn·nyhh_
the racetrack	**tor wyścigowy** _tohr vyhsh'·ch'ee·goh·vyh_
the stadium	**stadion** _stah·dyohn_
Where can I place a bet?	**Gdzie można postawić zakład?** _gdj'yeh mohzh·nah pohs·tah·veech' zah·kwaht_

Playing Sport

Where is/are...?	**Gdzie jest/są...?** _gdj'yeh yehst/sohm..._
the golf course	**pole golfowe** _poh·leh gohl·foh·veh_
the gym	**siłownia** _sh'ee·wohv·n'yah_
the park	**park** _pahrk_
the tennis courts	**korty tenisowe** _kohr·tyh teh·n'ee·soh·veh_
How much per...?	**Jaka jest stawka za...?** _yah·kah yehst stah·fkah zah..._
day	**dzień** _dj'yehn'_
hour	**godzinę** _goh·dj'ee·neh_
game	**mecz** _mehch_
round	**turę** _too·reh_

Can I rent [hire]...?	**Czy mogę wypożyczyć...?** _chyh_ _moh_•geh _vyh_•poh•_zhyh_•chyhch'
golf clubs	**kije do golfa** _kee_•yeh doh _gohl_•fah
equipment	**sprzęt** _spshehnt_
a racket	**rakietę** rah•_kyeh_•teh

At the Beach/Pool

Where's the beach/pool?	**Gdzie jest plaża/basen?** _gdj'yeh_ yehst _plah_•zhah/ _bah_•sehn
Is there...?	**Czy jest...?** chyh yehst...
a kiddie pool	**brodzik** _broh_•dj'eek
an indoor/ outdoor pool	**basen kryty/odkryty** _bah_•sehn kryh•tyh/oht•_kryh_•ty
a lifeguard	**ratownik** rah•_tohv_•n'eek
Is it safe to swim/ dive here?	**Można tu bezpiecznie pływać/skakać?** _mohzh_•nah too behs•_pyehch_•n'yeh pwyh•vach'/skah•kach'
Is it safe for children?	**Czy jest tu bezpiecznie dla dzieci?** chyh yehst too behs•_pyehch_•n'yeh dlah _dj'eh_•ch'ee
I'd like to rent [hire]...	**Chciałbym _m_ /Chciałabym _f_ wypożyczyć...** _hch'yahw_•byhm /hch'yah•wah•byhm vyh•poh•_zhyh_•chyhch'...
a deck chair	**leżak** _leh_•zhahk
diving equipment	**sprzęt do nurkowania** spshehnt doh noor•koh•_vah_•n'yah
a jet-ski	**skuter wodny** _skoo_•tehr _vohd_•nyh
a motorboat	**motorówkę** moh•toh•_roof_•keh
a rowboat	**łódkę wiosłową** _wood_•keh vyohs•_woh_•vohm
snorkeling equipment	**sprzęt do nurkowania z fajką** spshehnt doh noor•koh•_vah_•n'yah sfahy•kohm
a surfboard	**deskę surfingową** _dehs_•keh soor•feen•_goh_•vohm
a towel	**ręcznik** _rehn_•chn'eek

an umbrella	**parasol** pah·*rah*·sohl
waterskis	**narty wodne** *nahr*·tyh *vohd*·neh
a windsurfer	**deskę windsurfingową** *dehs*·keh *weend*·soor·feen·*goh*·vohm
For...hours.	**Na...godzin.** nah...*goh*·dj'een

Poland's sandy Baltic coast beaches are very popular during the summer months. Swim only in places that are marked **plaża strzeżona** (supervised beach) and have a **ratownik** (lifeguard); be sure to obey safety notices. The Mazury Lake District in the north-eastern part of Poland and the Greater Poland Lake District in the north-west are popular tourist destinations, especially for water sports lovers (swimming, sailing, windsurfing, fishing, diving and canoeing).

Winter Sports

A lift pass for a day/ five days, please.	**Poproszę jednodniowy/pięciodniowy skipass.** poh·*proh*·sheh yehd·noh·*dn'yoh*·vyh/ pyehn'·ch'yoh·*dn'yoh*·vyh *skee*·pahs
I'd like to rent [hire]...	**Chciałbym** *m* /**Chciałabym** *f* **wypożyczyć...** hch'yahw·byhm/hch'yah·wah·byhm fvyh·poh·*zhyh*·chych'...
boots	**buty narciarskie** *boo*·tyh nahr·*ch'yahr*·skyeh
cross-country skis	**biegówki** byeh·*goof*·kee
a helmet	**kask** kahsk
poles	**kijki** *keey*·kee
skates	**łyżwy** *wyhzh*·vyh
skis	**narty** *nahr*·tyh
a snowboard	**deskę snowboardową** *dehs*·keh snohw·bohr·*doh*·vohm
snowshoes	**rakiety śnieżne** rah·*kyeh*·tyh sh'n'*yehzh*·neh

These are too big/small.	**Te są za duże/małe.**	*teh sohm zah doo•zheh/ mah•weh*
Are there ski/ snowboard lessons?	**Czy jest nauka jazdy na nartach/snowboardzie?**	*chyh yehst nah•oo•kah yahz•dyh nah nahr•tahh/ snohw•bohr•dj'yeh*
I'm a beginner.	**Jestem początkujący m /początkująca f.**	*yehs•tehm poh•chohn•tkoo•yohn•tsyh/ poh•chohn•tkoo•yohn•tsah*
I'm experienced.	**Jestem zaawansowany m /zaawansowana f.**	*yehs•tehm zah•ah•vahn•soh•vah•nyh/ zah•ah•vahn•soh•vah•nah*
A trail [piste] map, please.	**Poproszę mapę tras.**	*poh•proh•sheh mah•peh trahs*

There are many ski resorts in the southern part of Poland, the most popular being Zakopane, Szczyrk and Wisła. The high Tatra Mountains offer excellent downhill skiing, and there are plenty of skiing opportunities on the lower slopes of many other mountains.

YOU MAY SEE...

WYCIĄG	drag lift
KOLEJKA LINOWA/GONDOLA	cable car/gondola
WYCIĄG KRZESEŁKOWY	chair lift
TRASA ŁATWA	novice
TRASA TRUDNA	intermediate
TRASA BARDZO TRUDNA	expert
TRASA ZAMKNIĘTA	trail [piste] closed
UWAGA LAWINY	caution, avalanches

Out in the Country

I'd like a map of…	**Poproszę mapę…**	poh•_proh_•sheh _mah_•peh…
this region	**tego regionu**	_teh_•goh reh•_gyoh_•noo
the walking routes	**tras pieszych**	trahs _pieh_•shyhh
the bike routes	**szlaków rowerowych**	_shlah_•koof roh•veh•_roh_•vyhh
the trails	**szlaków**	_shlah_•koof
Is it far?	**Czy to daleko?**	chyh toh dah•_leh_•koh
Is it easy/difficult?	**Czy to łatwa/trudna trasa?**	chyh toh _wah_•tvah/ _troo_•dnah _trah_•sah
Is it steep?	**Jest stromo?**	yehst _stroh_•moh
How far is it to…?	**Jak daleko jest do…?**	yahk dah•_leh_•koh yehst doh
I'm lost.	**Zgubiłem** m **/Zgubiłam** f **się.**	zgoo•_bee_•wehm/ zgoo•_bee_•wahm sh'yeh
Where's…?	**Gdzie jest…?**	gdj'yeh yehst…
the bridge	**most**	mohst
the cave	**jaskinia**	yahs•_kee_•n'yah
the cliff	**klif**	kleef
the farm	**gospodarstwo**	goh•spoh•_dahr_•stvoh
the field	**pole**	_poh_•leh
the forest	**las**	lahs
the lake	**jezioro**	yeh•_zh'yoh_•roh

the mountain	**góra** _goo_•rah
the national park	**park narodowy** pahrk nah•roh•_doh_•vyh
the nature reserve	**rezerwat przyrody** reh•_zehr_•vaht pshyh•_roh_•dyh
the overlook [viewpoint]	**punkt widokowy** poonkt vee•doh•_koh_•vyh
the park	**park** pahrk
the path	**ścieżka** sh'ch'_yesh_•kah
the peak	**szczyt** sh•chyht
the picnic area	**pole piknikowe** _poh_•leh peek•n'ee•_koh_•veh
the pond	**staw** stahv
the river	**rzeka** _zheh_•kah
the sea	**morze** _moh_•zheh
the (thermal) spring	**(gorące) źródło** (goh•_rohn_•tseh) zh'_rood_•woh
the stream	**strumień** _stroo_•myehn'
the valley	**dolina** doh•_lee_•nah
the vineyard	**winnica** veen•_nee_•tsah
the waterfall	**wodospad** voh•_dohs_•paht

Going Out

ESSENTIAL

What is there to do at night?	**Co można robić wieczorami?** *tsoh mozh·nah roh·beech' vyeh·choh·rah·mee*
Do you have a program of events?	**Czy jest program imprez?** *chyh yehst proh·grahm eem·prehs*
What's playing at the movies [cinema] today?	**Co dzisiaj grają w kinie?** *tsoh dj'ee·sh'yay grah·yohm fkee·n'yeh*
Where's...?	**Gdzie jest...?** *gdj'yeh yehst...*
the downtown area	**centrum** *tsehn·troom*
the bar	**bar** *bahr*
the dance club	**dyskoteka** *dyhs·koh·teh·kah*

Entertainment

Can you recommend...?	**Czy może pan polecić...?** *chyh moh·zheh pahn poh·leh·ch'eech'...*
a concert	**koncert** *kohn·tsehrt*
a movie	**film** *feelm*
an opera	**operę** *oh·peh·reh*
a play	**sztukę** *shtoo·keh*

Most hotels will have some information available in English about events around town. There are also culture magazines, such as **Kalejdoskop Kulturalny** (Cultural Kaleidoscope), which have weekly events listings, often provided in Polish and English. These are available at newsstands and bookstores.

When does it start/end?	**Kiedy to się zaczyna/kończy?** *kyeh•dyh toh sh'yeh zah•chyh•nah/kohn'•chyh*
I like…	**Lubię…** *loo•byeh…*
classical music	**muzykę poważną** *moo•zyh•keh poh•vahzh•nohm*
folk music	**muzykę ludową** *moo•zyh•keh loo•doh•vohm*
jazz	**jazz** *djehz*
pop music	**pop** *pohp*
rap	**rap** *rahp*
What's the dress code?	**Jaki strój obowiązuje?** *yah•kee strooy oh•boh•vyohn•zoo•yeh*

For Tickets, see page 19.

YOU MAY HEAR…

Prosimy o wyłączenie telefonów komórkowych. *proh•shee•myh oh vyh•wohn•cheh•n'yeh teh•leh•foh•noof koh•moor•koh•vyhh*

Turn off your cell [mobile] phones, please.

Nightlife

What is there to do at night?	**Co można robić wieczorami?** *tsoh mohzh•nah roh•beech' vyeh•choh•rah•mee*
Can you recommend…?	**Czy może pan polecić…?** *chyh moh•zheh pahn poh•leh•ch'eech'…*
a bar	**bar** *bahr*
a cabaret	**kabaret** *kah•bah•reht*
a casino	**kasyno** *kah•syh•noh*
a dance club	**dyskotekę** *dyhs•koh•teh•keh*

a gay club	**klub dla gejów** *kloop dlah <u>geh</u>•yoof*
a jazz club	**klub jazzowy** *kloop djeh•<u>zoh</u>•vyh*
a club with Polish music	**klub z polską muzyką** *kloop <u>spohls</u>•kohm moo•<u>zyh</u>•kohm*
Is there live music?	**Czy grają muzykę na żywo?** *chyh grah•yohm moo•<u>zyh</u>•keh nah <u>zhyh</u>•voh*
How do I get there?	**Jak tam dotrzeć?** *yahk tahm <u>doh</u>•tshehch'*
Is there a cover charge?	**Czy płaci się za wstęp?** *Chyh <u>pwah</u>•ch'ee sh'yeh zah vstehmp*
Let's go dancing.	**Chodźmy potańczyć.** *<u>hohch</u>'•myh poh•<u>tahn</u>'•chyhch'*
Is this area safe at night?	**Czy ta okolica jest bezpieczna w nocy?** *chyh tah oh•kho•lee•tsah yehst behs•py'eh•chnah vnoh•tsyh*

For The Dating Game, see page 107.

Dyskoteki (dance clubs) are popular throughout Poland. These feature a variety of music: dance, jazz, pop, etc. Prices are reasonable and many venues offer student discounts. At popular dance clubs you may need to make a reservation in advance.

Special Requirements

Business Travel

ESSENTIAL

I'm here on business.	**Przyjechałem** m **/Przyjechałam** f **tutaj służbowo.** pshyh•yeh•_hah_•wehm/pshyh•yeh•_hah_•wahm _too_•tahy swoozh•_boh_•voh
Here's my business card.	**To moja wizytówka.** toh _moh_•yah vee•zyh•_toof_•kah
Can I have your card?	**Mogę prosić o pana wizytówkę?** _moh_•geh _proh_•sh'eech' oh _pah_•nah vee•zyh•_toof_•keh
I have a meeting with...	**Mam spotkanie z...** mahm spoht•_kah_•n'yeh z...
Where's...?	**Gdzie jest...?** gdj'yeh yehst...
the business center	**centrum biznesowe** _tsehn_•troom beez•neh•_soh_•veh
the convention hall	**sala konferencyjna** _sah_•lah kohn•feh•rehn•_tsyhy_•nah
the meeting room	**sala spotkań** _sah_•lah _spoht_•kahn'

On Business

I'm here to attend...	**Przyjechałem** m **/Przyjechałam** f **na...** pshyh•yeh•_hah_•wehm/pshyh•yeh•_hah_•wahm nah...
a seminar	**seminarium** seh•mee•_nah_•ryoom
a conference	**konferencję** kohn•feh•_rehn_•tsyeh
a meeting	**spotkanie** spoht•_kah_•n'yeh
My name is...	**Nazywam się...** nah•_zyh_•vahm sh'yeh...
May I introduce my colleague...	**Proszę pozwolić mi przedstawić kolegę...** _proh_•sheh pohz•_voh_•leech' mee pshet•_stah_•veech' koh•_leh_•geh...
Pleasure to meet you.	**Miło mi pana poznać.** _mee_•woh mee _pah_•nah pohz•nahch'
I have a meeting with...	**Mam spotkanie z...** mahm spoht•_kah_•n'yeh z...

I have an appointment with…	**Jestem umówiony z…** _yehs_•tehm oo•moo•_vyoh_•nyh z…
I'm sorry I'm late.	**Przepraszam za spóźnienie.** psheh•_prah_•shahm zah spoozh'•_n'yeh_•n'yeh
I'd like an interpreter.	**Proszę o tłumacza.** _proh_•sheh oh twoo•_mah_•chah
You can contact me at the…Hotel.	**Można się ze mną kontaktować w hotelu…** _moh_•zhnah sh'yeh zeh mnohm kohn•tahk•_toh_•vach' f hoh•_teh_•loo…
I'm here until…	**Zostaję tu do…** zohs•_tah_•yeh too doh…
I need to…	**Muszę…** _moo_•sheh…
make a call	**zadzwonić** zah•_dzvoh_•n'eech'
make a photocopy	**zrobić ksero** _zroh_•beech' _kseh_•roh
send an e-mail	**wysłać e-mail** _vyh_•swahch' _ee_•meyl
send a fax	**wysłać fax** _vyh_•swahch' fahks
send a package (for next day delivery)	**wysłać paczkę (pocztą kurierską)** _vyh_•swahch' _pahch_•keh (_pohch_•tohm koor•_yehr_•skohm)

For Communications, see page 47.

Business people who meet for the first time shake hands and share their first names and surnames. Avoid clasping the hand of your partner with both hands. It is an accepted custom to exchange business cards at the first meeting. For subsequent meetings simply say: **dzień dobry/dobry wieczór** (hello/good evening) and shake hands. If a woman and a man meet, she is supposed to reach out her hand first. However, if two business people occupy different positions, it is always the senior one who reaches out his/her hand first.

YOU MAY HEAR...

Czy jest pan umówiony na spotkanie? *chyh yehst pahn oo•moo•vyoh•nyh nah spoht•kah•n'yeh*

Do you have an appointment?

Z kim? *skeem*

With whom?

Jest na zebraniu. *yehst nah zehb•rah•n'yoo*

He/She is in a meeting.

Proszę chwilę poczekać. *proh•sheh hvee•leh poh•cheh•kahch'*

One moment, please.

Proszę usiąść. *proh•sheh oo•sh'ohn'sh'ch'*

Have a seat.

Dziękuję za przybycie. *dj'yehn•koo•yeh zah pshyh•byh•ch'yeh*

Thank you for coming.

Traveling with Children

ESSENTIAL

Is there a discount for children?	**Czy jest zniżka dla dzieci?** *chyh yehst zn'eezh·kah dlah dj'yeh·ch'ee*
Can you recommend a babysitter?	**Czy może pan polecić opiekunkę do dzieci?** *chyh moh·zheh pahn poh·leh·ch'eech' oh·pyeh·koon·keh doh dj'yeh·ch'ee*
Do you have a child's seat/highchair?	**Mają państwo krzesełko dla dziecka/wysokie krzesełko?** *mah·yohm pahn'·stfoh ksheh·seh·wkoh dlah dj'yeh·tskah/vyh·soh·kyeh ksheh·seh·wkoh*
Where can I change the baby?	**Gdzie mogę przewinąć dziecko?** *gdj'yeh moh·geh psheh·vee·nohn'ch' dj'yehts·koh*

Out & About

Can you recommend something for kids?	**Czy może pan polecić coś dla dzieci?** *chyh moh•zheh pahn poh•leh•ch'eech' tsohsh' dlah dj'yeh•ch'ee*
Where's…?	**Gdzie jest…?** *gdj'yeh yehst…*
the amusement park	**wesołe miasteczko** *veh•soh•weh myahs•teh•chkoh*
the arcade	**salon gier** *sah•lohn gyehr*
the kiddie [paddling] pool	**brodzik** *broh•dj'eek*
the park	**park** *pahrk*
the playground	**plac zabaw** *plahts zah•bahf*
the zoo	**zoo** *zoh•oh*
Are children allowed?	**Czy można wchodzić z dziećmi?** *chyh mohzh•nah fhoh•dj'eech' zdj'yehch'•mee*
Is it safe for kids?	**Czy to jest bezpieczne dla dzieci?** *chyh toh yehst behs•pyehch•neh dlah dj'yeh•ch'ee*
Is it suitable for… year olds?	**Czy to jest odpowiednie dla…-latków?** *chyh toh yehst oht•poh•vyehd•n'yeh dlah…-laht•koof*

For Numbers, see page 171.

YOU MAY HEAR…

Jakie słodkie! *yah•kyeh swoht•kyeh*	How cute!
Jak ma na imię? *yahk mah nah ee•myeh*	What's his/her name?
Ile ma lat? *ee•leh mah laht*	How old is he/she?

Baby Essentials

Do you have…?	**Czy mają państwo…?** *chyh mah•yohm pahn'•stfoh…*
a baby bottle	**butelkę ze smoczkiem** *boo•tehl•keh zeh smohch•kyehm*
baby wipes	**wilgotne chusteczki pielęgnacyjne** *veel•goht•neh hoos•tehch•kee pyeh•lehn•gnah•tsyhy•neh*
a car seat	**fotelik samochodowy** *foh•teh•leek sah•moh•hoh•doh•vyh*
a child's seat/ highchair	**krzesełko dla dziecka/wysokie krzesełko** *ksheh•seh•wkoh dlah dj'yeh•tskah/vyh•soh•kyeh ksheh•seh•wkoh*
a crib/cot	**łóżko składane/łóżeczko dziecięce** *woo•shkoh skwah•dah•neh/woo•zhehch•koh dj'yeh•ch'ehn•tseh*
diapers [nappies]	**pieluszki** *pyeh•loosh•kee*
a pacifier [dummy]	**smoczek** *smoh•chehk*
a playpen	**kojec** *koh•yehts*
a stroller [pushchair]	**wózek spacerowy** *voo•zehk spah•tseh•roh•vyh*
Can I breastfeed the baby here?	**Czy mogę tutaj karmić dziecko piersią?** *chyh moh•geh too•tay kahr•meech' dj'yehts•koh pyehr•sh'yohm*

| Where can I change the baby? | **Gdzie mogę przewinąć dziecko?** *gdj'yeh moh•geh psheh•vee•nohn'ch' dj'yehts•koh* |

For Dining with Children, see page 62.

Babysitting

Can you recommend a babysitter?	**Czy może pan polecić opiekunkę do dzieci?** *chyh moh•zheh pahn poh•leh•ch'eech' oh•pyeh•koon•keh doh dj'yeh•ch'ee*
What's the charge?	**Jaka jest opłata?** *yah•kah yehst oh•pwah•tah*
I'll be back by…	**Przyjdę za…** *pshyhy•deh zah…*
I can be reached at…	**Można do mnie dzwonić na numer…** *moh•zhnah doh mn'yeh dzvoh•n'eech' nah noo•mehr…*

For Time, see page 173.

Health & Emergency

Can you recommend a pediatrician?	**Czy może pan polecić pediatrę?** *chyh moh•zheh pahn poh•leh•ch'eech' peh•dyaht•reh*
My child is allergic to…	**Moje dziecko ma uczulenie na…** *moh•yeh dj'yeh•tskoh mah oo•choo•leh•n'yeh nah…*
My child is missing.	**Moje dziecko się zgubiło.** *moh•yeh dj'yeh•tskoh sh'yeh zgoo•bee•woh*
Have you seen a boy/girl?	**Czy widział pan chłopca/dziewczynkę?** *chyh vee•dj'yahw pahn hwohp•tsah/dj'yehv•chyhn•keh*

For Meals & Cooking, see page 65.

For Health, see page 156.

For Police, see page 154.

Disabled Travelers

ESSENTIAL

Is there...?	**Czy jest...?** *chyh yehst...*
access for the disabled	**dostęp dla niepełnosprawnych** *dohs·tehmp dlah n'yeh·pehw·noh·sprahv·nyhh*
a wheelchair ramp	**podjazd dla wózków inwalidzkich** *pohd·yahst dlah voos·koof een·vah·leets·keeh*
a disabled-accessible toilet	**toaleta dla niepełnosprawnych** *toh·ah·leh·tah dlah n'yeh·pew·noh·sprahv·nyhh*
I need...	**Potrzebuję...** *poh·tsheh·boo·yeh...*
assistance	**pomocy** *poh·moh·tsyh*
an elevator [lift]	**windy** *veen·dyh*
a ground-floor room	**pokoju na parterze** *poh·koh·yoo nah pahr·teh·zheh*

Asking for Assistance

I'm disabled.	**Jestem nepełnosprawny** *m* **/niepełnosprawna** *f* *yehs·tehm n'yeh·pehw·noh·sprahv·nyh/ n'yeh·pehw·noh·sprahv·nah*
I'm deaf.	**Jestem głuchy** *m* **/głucha** *f.* *yehs·tehm gwoo·hyh/ gwoo·hah*
I'm visually/hearing impaired.	**Niedowidzę./Niedosłyszę.** *n'yeh·doh·vee·dzeh/ n'yeh·doh·swyh·sheh*
I'm unable to walk far/ use the stairs.	**Nie mogę dużo chodzić/chodzić po schodach.** *n'yeh moh·geh doo·zhoh hoh·dj'eech'/hoh·dj'eech' poh s·hoh·dahh*
Can I bring my wheelchair?	**Czy mogę być na wózku inwalidzkim?** *chyh moh·geh byhch' nah voos·koo een·vah·leets·keem*

Are guide dogs permitted?	**Czy mogę być z psem przewodnikiem?** *chyh moh•geh byhch' spsehm psheh•vohd•n'ee•kyem*
Can you help me?	**Czy może mi pan pomóc?** *chyh moh•zheh mee pahn poh•moots*
Please open/hold the door.	**Proszę otworzyć/przytrzymać drzwi.** *proh•sheh oht•foh•zhyhch'/pshyh•tshyh•mahch' djvee*

For Emergencies, see page 153.

In an Emergency

Emergencies

ESSENTIAL

Help!	**Pomocy!** *poh·moh·tsyh*
Go away!	**Proszę odejść!** *proh·sheh oh·deysh'ch'*
Leave me alone!	**Zostaw mnie w spokoju!** *zoh·stahf mn'yeh fspoh·koh·yoo*
Stop thief!	**Łapać złodzieja!** *wah·pach' zwoh·dj'yeh·yah*
Get a doctor!	**Wezwijcie lekarza!** *vez·veey·ch'yeh leh·kah·zhah*
Fire!	**Pali się!** *pah·lee sh'yeh*
I'm lost.	**Zgubiłem się** *m* /**Zgubiłam się** *f.* *zgoo·bee·wehm sh'yeh/zgoo·bee·wahm sh'yeh*
Can you help me?	**Czy może mi pan pomóc?** *chyh moh·zheh mee pahn poh·moots*

YOU MAY HEAR…

Proszę wypełnić ten formularz. *proh·sheh vyh·pehw·n'eech' tehn fohr·moo·lash'*	Please fill out this form.
Poproszę dowód tożsamości. *poh·proh·sheh doh·voot tohsh'·sah·mohsh'·ch'ee*	Your identification, please.
Gdzie/Kiedy to się stało? *gdj'eh/kyeh·dyh toh sh'yeh stah·woh*	When/Where did it happen?
Jak on/ona wygląda? *yahk ohn/oh·nah vyh·glohn·dah*	What does he/she look like?
Proszę tu poczekać. *proh·sheh too poh·cheh·kahch'*	Please wait here.
Jak można się z panem skontaktować? *yahk moh·zhnah sh'yeh spah·nehm skohn·tahk·toh·vahch'*	How may we contact you?

Police

ESSENTIAL

Call the police!	**Wezwijcie policję!** vez·_veey_·ch'yeh poh·_leets_·yeh
Where's the police station?	**Gdzie jest komisariat?** gdj'yeh yehst koh·mee·_sahr_·yaht
There has been an accident/attack.	**Zdarzył się wypadek/napad.** _zdah_·zhyhw sh'yeh vyh·_pah_·dehk/_nah_·paht
My child is missing.	**Moje dziecko się zgubiło.** _moh_·yeh _dj'yeh_·tskoh sh'yeh zgoo·_bee_·woh
I need...	**Potrzebuję...** poh·tsh'eh·_boo_·yeh...
an interpreter	**tłumacza** twoo·_mah_·chah
to contact my lawyer	**skontaktować się z moim prawnikiem** skohn·tah·_ktoh_·vahch' sh'yeh _zmoh_·eem prah·_vn'ee_·kyehm
to make a phone call	**zatelefonować** zah·teh·leh·foh·_noh_·vach'
I'm innocent.	**Jestem niewinny m /niewinna f.** _yeh_·stehm n'yeh·_veen_·nyh/n'yeh·_veen_·nah
It was an accident.	**To był wypadek.** toh byhw vyh·_pah_·dehk

Crime & Lost Property

I want to report...	**Chcę zgłosić...** htseh _zgwoh_·sh'eech'...
a mugging	**napad** _nah_·paht
a rape	**gwałt** gvahwt
a theft	**kradzież** _krah_·djyesh
I've been robbed/ mugged.	**Okradli/Napadli mnie.** oh·_krah_·dlee/nah·_pah_·dlee mn'yeh

I've lost my…	**Zgubiłem…***m* /**Zgubiłam…***f* zgoo·*bee*·wehm…/ zgoo·*bee*·wahm…
My…has been stolen.	**Ukradli mi…** oo·*krah*·dlee mee…
luggage	**bagaż** _bah_·gahsh
backpack [rucksack]	**plecak** _pleh_·tsahk
bicycle	**rower** roh·vehr
camera	**aparat fotograficzny** ah·*pah*·raht foh·toh·grah·*feech*·nyh
video camera	**kamerę** kah·*meh*·reh
(rental [hire]) car	**(wynajęty) samochód** (vyh·nah·*yen*·tyh) sah·*moh*·hoot
laptop	**laptop** _lahp_·tohp
credit card	**kartę kredytową** _kahr_·teh kreh·dyh·_toh_·vohm
cell [mobile] phone	**komórkę** koh·_moor_·keh
jewelry	**biżuterię** bee·zhoo·_tehr_·yeh
money	**pieniądze** pyeh·*n'yohn*·dzeh
passport	**paszport** _pahsh_·pohrt
purse [handbag]	**torebkę** toh·_rehp_·keh
travelers checks	**czeki podróżne** _cheh_·kee pohd·_roozh_·neh
wallet	**portfel** _pohrt_·fehl
I need a police report.	**Muszę mieć raport z policji.** _moo_·sheh myehch' _rah_·pohrt spoh·_leets_·yee
Where is the British/ American/Irish embassy?	**Gdzie jest ambasada brytyjska/amerykańska/ irlandzka?** gdj'yeh yehst ahm·bah·_sah_·dah bryh·_tyhy_·skah/ ah·meh·ryh·_kahn'_·skah eer·_lahnt_skah

In an emergency, dial: **112** for the police
998 for the fire brigade
999 for the ambulance.

Health

ESSENTIAL

I'm sick [ill].	**Jestem chory m /chora f.** *yeh·stehm hoh·ryh / hoh·rah*
I don't feel well.	**Źle się czuję.** *zh'leh sh'yeh choo·yeh*
Is there an English-speaking doctor?	**Czy jest tu lekarz mówiący po angielsku?** *chyh yehst too leh·kahsh moo·vyohn·tsyh poh ahn·gyehls·koo*
It hurts here.	**Boli mnie tutaj.** *boh·lee mn'yeh too·tay*
I have a stomachache.	**Boli mnie brzuch.** *boh·lee mn'yeh bzhooh*

Finding a Doctor

Can you recommend a doctor/dentist?	**Czy może pan polecić lekarza/dentystę?** *chyh moh·zheh pahn poh·leh·ch'eech' leh·kah·zhah/ dehn·tyh·steh*
Could the doctor come to see me here?	**Czy lekarz może przyjść mnie zbadać tutaj?** *chy leh·kash moh·zheh pshyhysh'ch' mn'yeh zbah·dach' too·tay*

I need an English-speaking doctor.	**Potrzebuję lekarza mówiącego po angielsku.** *poht·sheh·boo·yeh leh·kah·zhah moo·vyohn·tseh·goh poh ahn·gyehls·koo*
What are the office [surgery] hours?	**Jakie są godziny przyjęć?** *yahk·yeh sohm goh·dj·ee·nyh pshyh·yehnch'*
Can I make an appointment...?	**Czy mogę zamówić wizytę...?** *chyh moh·geh zah·moo·veech' vee·zyh·teh...*
for today	**na dzisiaj** *nah dj·ee·sh'yahy*
for tomorrow	**na jutro** *nah yoo·troh*
as soon as possible	**na jak najbliższy termin** *nah yahk nahy·bleesh·shyh tehr·meen*
It's urgent.	**To jest pilne.** *toh yest peel·neh*
It's an emergency.	**To nagły wypadek.** *toh nah·gwyh vyh·pah·dehk*

Symptoms

I'm...	**Mam...** *mahm...*
bleeding	**krwotok** *krfoh·tohk*
constipated	**zaparcie** *zah·pahr·ch'yeh*
dizzy	**zawroty głowy** *zah·vroh·tyh gwoh·vyh*
nauseous	**mdłości** *mdwosh'·ch'ee*
I'm vomiting.	**Wymiotuję.** *vyh·myoh·too·yeh*
It hurts here.	**Boli mnie tutaj.** *boh·lee mn'yeh too·tay*
I have...	**Mam...** *mahm...*
an allergic reaction	**reakcję alergiczną** *reh·ahk·tsyeh ah·lehr·geech·nohm*
chest pain	**bóle w klatce piersiowej** *boo·leh f klaht·tseh pyehr·sh'yoh·vey*
a fever	**gorączkę** *goh·rohnch·keh*
pain	**bóle** *boo·leh*
a rash	**wysypkę** *vyh·syhp·keh*
a sprain	**zwichnięcie** *zvee·hn'yehn'·ch'yeh*

some swelling	**opuchliznę** *oh-poo-hleez-neh*
sunstroke	**udar słoneczny** *oo-dahr swoh-nehch-nyh*
I have...	**Boli mnie...** *boh-lee mn'yeh...*
an earache	**ucho** *oo-hoh*
a stomachache	**brzuch** *bzhooh*
a headache	**głowa** *gwoh-vah*
I've been sick for...days.	**Źle się czuję od...dni.** *zh'leh sh'yeh choo-yeh oht...dn'yee*

For Numbers, see page 171.

Conditions

I'm...	**Mam...** *mahm...*
anemic	**anemię** *ah-neh-myeh*
asthmatic	**astmę** *ahst-meh*
diabetic	**cukrzycę** *tsook-shyh-tseh*
epileptic	**Mam padaczkę** *mahm pah-dah-chkeh*
I'm allergic to antibiotics/ penicillin.	**Mam uczulenie na antybiotyki/penicylinę.** *Mahm oo-choo-leh-n'yeh nah ahn-tyh-byoh-tyh-kee/ peh-nee-tsyh-lee-neh*
I have arthritis.	**Mam artretyzm.** *mahm ahr-treh-tyhsm*
I have high/low blood pressure.	**Mam wysokie/niskie ciśnienie.** *mahm vyh-soh-kyeh/nees-kyeh ch'eesh'-n'yeh-n'yeh*
I have a heart condition.	**Choruję na serce.** *hoh-roo-yeh na sehr-tseh*
I'm on...	**Zażywam...** *zah-zhyh-vahm...*

For Meals & Cooking, see page 65.

YOU MAY HEAR...

W czym problem? *fchyhm proh•blehm*
What's wrong?

Gdzie boli? *gdj'yeh boh•lee*
Where does it hurt?

Czy boli tutaj? *chyh boh•lee too•tay*
Does it hurt here?

Czy przyjmuje pan regularnie leki?
chyh pshyhy•moo•yeh pahn reh•goo•lahr•n'yeh leh•kee
Are you on medication?

Czy jest pan na coś uczulony? *chyh yehst pahn nah tsosh' oo•choo•loh•nyh*
Are you allergic to anything?

Proszę otworzyć usta. *proh•sheh oht•foh•zhyhch' oo•stah*
Please open your mouth.

Oddychać głęboko. *ohd•dyh•hach' gwehm•boh•koh*
Breathe deeply.

Pójdzie pan do szpitala. *pooy•dj'yeh pahn doh shpee•tah•lah*
You must go to the hospital.

Treatment

Do I need a prescription/ medicine?	**Czy potrzebuję lekarstwa/recepty?** *chyh poh•tzheh•boo•yeh leh•kahrs•tfah/ reh•tsehp•tyh*
Can you prescribe a generic drug [unbranded medication]?	**Czy mogę prosić o przepisanie leku generycznego [niemarkowego]** *chyh moh•geh proh•sh'eech' oh psh'eh•pee•sah•nyeh leh•koo geh•neh•ryhch•neh•goh (n'ye•mahr•koh•veh•goh)*
Where can I get it?	**Gdzie to mogę dostać?** *Gdj'yeh toh moh•geh doh•stahch'*

For Pharmacy, see page 162.

Hospital

Please notify my family.	**Proszę zawiadomić moją rodzinę.** _proh·sheh zah·vyah·doh·meech' moh·yohm roh·dj'ee·neh_
I'm in pain.	**Boli mnie.** _boh·lee mn'yeh_
I need a doctor/nurse.	**Potrzebuję lekarza/pielęgniarki.** _poh·tsheh·boo·yeh leh·kah·zhah/ pyeh·lehng·n'yahr·kee_
When are visiting hours?	**Jakie są godziny odwiedzin?** _yah·kyeh sohm goh·dj'ee·nyh ohd·vyeh·dj'een_
I'm visiting...	**Odwiedzam...** _ohd·vyeh·dzahm..._

YOU MAY HEAR...

Musimy zrobić rentgen. _moo·sh'ee·myh zroh·beech' rehnt·gehn_	We must X-ray you.
Proszę podpisać zgodę na operację. _proh·sheh poht·pee·sahch' zgoh·deh nah oh·peh·rah·tsyeh_	Please sign the consent for surgery.

Dentist

I've lost a filling.	**Wypadła mi plomba.** _vyh·pahd·wah mee plohm·bah_
I've lost a tooth.	**Wypadł mi ząb.** _vyh·pahdw mee zohmp_
I have a toothache.	**Boli mnie ząb.** _boh·lee mn'yeh zohmp_
Can you fix this denture?	**Czy da się naprawić tę protezę?** _chyh dah sh'yeh nah·prah·veech' teh proh·teh·zeh_
I'd like an anesthetic.	**Poproszę znieczulenie.** _poh·proh·sheh zn'yeh·choo·leh·n'yeh_

Gynecologist

I have menstrual cramps/ a vaginal infection.	**Mam bóle miesiączkowe/infekcję pochwy.** *mahm boo•leh myeh•sh'yohn•chkoh•veh/ een•fehk•tsyeh poh•hfyh*
I missed my period.	**Spóźnia mi się okres.** *spoo•zh'n'yah mee sh'yeh ohk•rehs*
I'm on the pill.	**Biorę pigułki antykoncepcyjne.** *byoh•reh pee•goow•kee ahn•tyh•kohn•tsep•tsyhy•neh*
I'm (not) pregnant.	**(Nie) Jestem w ciąży.** *(n'yeh) yehs•tehm fch'yohn•zhyh*
I haven't had my period for…months.	**Nie miałam okresu od…miesięcy.** *n'yeh myah•wahm oh•kreh•soo oht…myeh•sh'yen•tsyh*

For Numbers, see page 171.

Optician

I've lost…	**Zgubiłem m /Zgubiłam f …** *zgoo•bee•wehm/ zgoo•bee•wahm …*
a contact lens	**soczewkę kontaktową** *soh•chehf•keh kohn•tahk•toh•vohm*
my glasses	**okulary** *oh•koo•lah•ryh*
a lens	**soczewkę** *soh•chef•keh*

Payment & Insurance

How much?	**Ile to kosztuje?** *ee•leh toh kohsh•too•yeh*
Can I pay by credit card?	**Czy mogę zapłacić kartą kredytową?** *chyh moh•geh zah•pwah•ch'eech' kahr•tohm kreh•dyh•toh•vohm*
I have insurance.	**Mam ubezpieczenie.** *mam oo•behs•pyeh•che•n'yeh*
Can I have a receipt for my insurance?	**Czy mogę dostać pokwitowanie dla mojego ubezpieczenia?** *chyh moh•geh dohs•tach' poh•kfee•toh•vah•n'yeh dlah moh•yeh•goh oo•behs•pyeh•cheh•n'yah*

Pharmacy

ESSENTIAL

Where's the nearest (24-hour) pharmacy?	**Gdzie jest najbliższa apteka (całodobowa)?** *gdj'yeh yest nay·bleesh·sha ah·pteh·kah (tsah·woh·doh·boh·vah)*
What time does the pharmacy open/close?	**O której otwierają/zamykają aptekę?** *oh ktoo·rey oht·fyeh·rah·yohm/zah·myh·kah· yohm ah·pteh·keh*
What would you recommend for…?	**Co może mi pan polecić na…?** *tsoh moh·zheh mee pahn poh·leh·ch'eech' nah…*
How much do I take?	**Ile mam brać?** *ee·leh mahm brahch'*
Can you fill this prescription?	**Czy możecie zrealizować tę receptę?** *chyh moh·zheh·ch'yeh zreh·ah·lee·zoh·vach' teh reh·tsehp·teh*
I'm allergic to…	**Mam uczulenie na…** *mahm oo·choo·leh·n'yeh nah…*

Pharmacies in Poland are easily identifiable by the sign **APTEKA** and a cross. Hours are generally from 9:00 a.m. to 6:00 p.m.; some operate around the clock. The names and locations of these 24-hour pharmacies are posted on the doors and windows of other pharmacies. You will need a prescription for drugs not available over the counter. Most pharmacies nowadays sell toiletries and cosmetics, too.

What to Take

I'd like some medicine for…	**Poproszę lekarstwo na…**	poh·*proh*·sheh leh·*kahrs*·tfoh nah…
a cold	**przeziębienie**	psheh·zh'yehm·*byeh*·n'yeh
a cough	**kaszel**	*kah*·shehl
a headache	**ból głowy**	boohl *gwoh*·vyh
diarrhea	**biegunkę**	byeh·*goon*·keh
the flu	**grypę**	*gryh*·peh
motion [travel] sickness	**chorobę lokomocyjną**	hoh·*roh*·beh loh·koh·moh·*tsyhy*·nohm
a sore throat	**ból gardła**	bool *gahr*·dwah
a toothache	**ból zęba**	boohl zehm·bah
an upset stomach	**rozstrój żołądka**	*rohs*·strooy zhoh·*wohnt*·kah
How much should I take?	**Ile mam wziąć?**	*ee*·leh mahm vzh'yonch'
How often should I take it?	**Jak często mam to brać?**	yahk *chehn*·stoh mahm toh brahch'
Is it suitable for children?	**Czy to jest odpowiednie dla dzieci?**	chyh toh yest oht·poh·*vyehd*·n'yeh dlah *dj'yeh*·ch'ee
I'm on…	**Biorę…**	*byoh*·reh…
Are there side effects?	**Czy są jakieś efekty uboczne?**	chyh sohm *yah*·kyesh' eh·*fehk*·tyh oo·*bohch*·neh

YOU MAY SEE...

RAZ/TRZY RAZY DZIENNIE	once/three times a day
TABLETKA	tablet
KROPLA	drop
ŁYŻECZKA	teaspoon
PRZED POSIŁKIEM	before meals
PO/W TRAKCIE POSIŁKU	after/with meals
NA CZCZO	on an empty stomach
POŁYKAĆ W CAŁOŚCI	swallow whole
MOŻE POWODOWAĆ SENNOŚĆ	may cause drowsiness
WYŁĄCZNIE DO UŻYTKU ZEWNĘTRZNEGO	for external use only

Basic Supplies

I'd like...	**Poproszę...** poh·_proh_·sheh...
acetaminophen [paracetamol]	**paracetamol** pah·rah·tseh·_tah_·mohl
antiseptic cream	**krem aseptyczny** krehm ah·sehp·_tyhch_·nyh
aspirin	**aspirynę** ah·spee·_ryh_·neh
a bandage	**bandaż** _bahn_·dahzh
a comb	**grzebień** _gzheh_·byen'
condoms	**prezerwatywy** preh·zehr·vah·_tyh_·vyh
contact lens solution	**płyn do soczewek kontaktowych** pwyhn doh soh·_cheh_·vehk kohn·tahk·_toh_·vyh
deodorant	**dezodorant** deh·zoh·_doh_·rahnt
a hairbrush	**szczotkę do włosów** _shchoht_·keh doh _vwoh_·soof
hair spray	**lakier do włosów** _lah_·kyehr doh _vwoh_·soof
ibuprofen	**ibuprofen** ee·boo·_proh_·fehn
insect repellent	**środek na owady** _sh'roh_·dehk nah oh·_vah_·dyh
lotion	**balsam** _bahl_·sahm

a nail file	**pilnik do paznokci** _peel·n'eek doh pahz·nohk·ch'ee_
painkillers	**środki przeciwbólowe** _sh'roht·kee psheh·ch'eef·boo·loh·veh_
a (disposable) razor	**(jednorazową) maszynkę do golenia** _(yehd·noh·rah·zoh·vohm) mah·shyhn·keh doh goh·leh·n'yah_
razor blades	**żyletki** _zhyh·leht·kee_
sanitary napkins [towels]	**podpaski** _poht·pahs·kee_
shampoo/conditioner	**szampon/odżywkę** _shahm·pohn/ohd·zhyhf·keh_
soap	**mydło** _myh·dwoh_
sunscreen	**krem do opalania** _krehm doh oh·pah·lah·n'yah_
tampons	**tampony** _tahm·poh·nyh_
tissues	**chusteczki papierowe** _hoos·tech·kee pahp·yeh·roh·veh_
toilet paper	**papier toaletowy** _pah·pyehr toh·ah·leh·toh·vyh_
a toothbrush	**szczoteczkę do zębów** _shchoh·tech·keh doh zehm·boof_
toothpaste	**pastę do zębów** _pah·steh doh zehm·boof_

For Baby Essentials, see page 148.

Grammar

> In Polish, there are two forms for you: **ty** (singular) and **wy**
> (plural). These are used when talking to relatives, close friends
> and children as well as among young people. When addressing
> someone in a formal situation use **pan** (Mr/sir), **pani** (Mrs/Ms/ma'am
> [madam]) or **państwo** (for groups).

Regular Verbs

Polish verbs are conjugated based on person, number, tense and gender.
Following are the present, past and future forms of the verbs **robić** (to do) and
mieć (to have).

The following abbreviations are used in this section: sing. = singular; pl. =
plural; fml. = formal;

ROBIĆ (to do)		Present	Past	Future
I	**ja**	robię	robi**łem** m robi**łam** f	będ**ę** robić
you	**ty**	robisz	robi**łeś** m robi**łaś** f	będzie**sz** robić
he/sir	**on/ pan**	robi	robi**ł** m	będzie robić
she/madam	**ona/ pani**	robi	robi**ła** f	będzie robić
it	**ono**	robi	robi**ło**	będzie robić
we	**my**	robi**my**	robi**liśmy** m robi**łyśmy** f	będzie**my** robić

you	**wy**	rob**icie**	robi**liście** m robi**łyście** f	będziecie robić
they	**oni** m / robią **one** f / **państwo**		robi**li** m robi**ły** f	będą robić
(pl. fml.)				

MIEĆ (to have)		Present	Past	Future
I	**ja**	mam	mia**łem** m mia**łam** f	będę mieć
you	**ty**	masz	mia**łeś** m mia**łaś** f	będzi**esz** mieć
he/sir	**on/** **pan**	ma	miał m	będzie mieć
she/madam	**ona/** **pani**	ma	mia**ła** f	będzie mieć
it	**ono**	ma	miało	będzie mieć
we	**my**	mamy	mieli**śmy** m miały**śmy** f	będzi**emy** mieć
you	**wy**	macie	mieli**ście** m miały**ście** f	będzi**ecie** mieć
they	**oni** m / mają **one** f / **państwo**		miel**i** m miał**y** f	będą mieć
(pl. fml.)				

Irregular Verbs

Irregular verbs are not conjugated by following the normal rules. Following are two common irregular verbs, **być** (to be) and **iść** (to go):

BYĆ (to be)		Present	Past	Future
I	**ja**	jestem	byłem m byłam f	będę
you	**ty**	jesteś	byłeś m	będziesz

			byłaś f	
he/sir	on/ pan	jest	był m	będzie
she/madam	ona/ pani	jest	była f	będzie
it	ono	jest	było	będzie
we	my	jesteśmy	byliśmy m byłyśmy f	będziemy
you	wy	jesteście	byliście m byłyście f	będziecie
they (pl. fml.)	oni m / one f / państwo	są	byli m były f	będą

IŚĆ (to go)		Present	Past	Future
I	ja	idę	szedłem m szłam f	będę iść
you	ty	idziesz	szedłeś m szłaś f	będziesz iść
he/sir	on/ pan	idzie	szedł m	będzie iść
she/madam	ona /pani	idzie	szła f	będzie iść
it	ono	idzie	szło	będzie iść
we	my	idziemy	szliśmy m szłyśmy f	będziemy iść
you	wy	idziecie	szliście m szłyście f	będziecie iść
they (pl. fml.)	oni m / one f / państwo	idą	szli m szły f	będą iść

Nouns

Nouns in Polish are either masculine, feminine or neuter. Masculine nouns usually end in a consonant. Feminine nouns usually end in **–a** or, less often, **–i**. Neuter nouns end in **–ę** or **–o**. Most masculine and feminine nouns, when plural, end in **–y** or in **–i**; most neuter nouns in **–a**.

The endings of nouns vary according to their role in the sentence. There are seven different cases (roles) in both the singular and plural.

There are no articles (a, an, the) in Polish.

Word Order

Word order in Polish is usually as in English, i.e., subject-verb-object. However, word order can be more flexible, because the word endings indicate the role of each word in the sentence.

Example: **Ania dała książkę Markowi.** = **Ania dała Markowi książkę.**
= **Ania Markowi dała książkę.** (Ania gave Marek a book.)

To ask a question in Polish:

1. use **czy**

Example: **Czy to pan Kowalski?** Is it Mr. Kowalski?

2. add rising intonation to an affirmative statement

Example: **Pan Kowalski?** Mr. Kowalski?

3. use question words

gdzie, kiedy, kto, co where, when, who, what

Example: **Gdzie jesteś?** Where are you?

Kiedy wrócisz? When are you coming back?

Co będziemy robić? What are we going to do?

Negation

To form a negative sentence, add **nie** (not) before the verb. Note that noun endings may change.

Example: **Mam bilet.** I have a ticket.

Nie mam biletu. I don't have a ticket.

Imperatives

Imperative sentences are formed by adding the appropriate ending to the verb stem.

Example: Go!

you	**ty**	**Idź!**
he/sir	**on/pan**	**Niech idzie!**
she/madam	**ona/pani**	**Niech idzie!**
it	**ono**	**Niech idzie!**
we	**my**	**Idźmy!**
you	**wy**	**Idźcie!**
they (pl. fml.)	**oni** *m* /**one** *f*	**Niech idą!**
		Niech państwo idą

Adjectives

Adjectives must agree in gender, number and case with the nouns they modify. Masculine adjectives usually end in **–y** or **–i**. The feminine and neuter endings are –a and –e, respectively.

Example: **To duży** *m* **dom** *m*. This is a big house.

To duża *f* **szkoła** *f*. This is a big school.

To duże dziecko. This is a big child.

Comparative & Superlative

The comparative is usually formed by adding **–szy** *m* /**–sza** *f* /**–sze** *(neuter)* and the superlative by adding **naj...–szy** *m* /**–sza** *f* /**–sze** *(neuter)*.

Example:

tani (cheap) **tańszy** **najtańszy**

Less common adjectives often use the complex comparative and superlative form:

comparative = **bardziej** (more) + adjective

superlative = **najbardziej** (the most) + adjective

Example:

tradycyjny (traditional)   **bardziej tradycyjny**   **najbardziej tradycyjny**

Adverbs

Some adverbs in Polish are formed from adjectives by adding the ending **–o**, but there is no fixed rule.

Example: **To szybki samochód.** This is a fast car. (adjective)

Robert jeździ szybko samochodem. Robert drives his car fast. (adverb)

Numbers

ESSENTIAL

0	**zero** *zeh·roh*
1	**jeden** *yeh·dehn*
2	**dwa** *dvah*
3	**trzy** *tshyh*
4	**cztery** *chteh·ryh*
5	**pięć** *pyehn'ch'*
6	**sześć** *shehsh'ch'*
7	**siedem** *sh'yeh·dehm*
8	**osiem** *oh·sh'yehm*
9	**dziewięć** *dj'yeh·vyehn'ch'*
10	**dziesięć** *dj'yeh·sh'yehn'ch'*
11	**jedenaście** *yeh·deh·nahsh'·ch'yeh*
12	**dwanaście** *dvah·nahsh'·ch'yeh*
13	**trzynaście** *tshyh·nahsh'·ch'yeh*

14	**czternaście** *chtehr·nahsh'·ch'yeh*
15	**piętnaście** *pyeht·nahsh'·ch'yeh*
16	**szesnaście** *shehs·nahsh'·ch'yeh*
17	**siedemnaście** *sh'yehdehm·nahsh'·ch'yeh*
18	**osiemnaście** *oh·sh'yehm·nahsh'·ch'yeh*
19	**dziewiętnaście** *dj'yeh·vyeht·nahsh'·ch'yeh*
20	**dwadzieścia** *dvah·dj'yehsh'·ch'yah*
21	**dwadzieścia jeden** *dvah·dj'yehsh'·ch'yah yeh·dehn*
22	**dwadzieścia dwa** *dvah·dj'yehsh'·ch'yah dvah*
30	**trzydzieści** *tshyh·dj'yehsh'·ch'ee*
40	**czterdzieści** *chtehr·dj'yehsh'·ch'ee*
50	**pięćdziesiąt** *pyehn'·dj'yeh·sh'yohnt*
60	**sześćdziesiąt** *shehsh'·dj'yeh·sh'yont*
70	**siedemdziesiąt** *sh'yeh·dehm·dj'yeh·sh'yohnt*
80	**osiemdziesiąt** *oh·sh'yehm·dj'yeh·sh'yohnt*
90	**dziewięćdziesiąt** *dj'eh·vyen'·dj'yeh·sh'ohnt*
100	**sto** *stoh*
101	**sto jeden** *stoh·yeh·dehn*
200	**dwieście** *dvyehsh'·ch'yeh*
500	**pięćset** *pyehnch'·seht*
1,000	**tysiąc** *tyh·sh'yohnts*
10,000	**dziesięć tysięcy** *dj'yeh·sh'yehn'ch' tyh·sh'yen·tsyh*
1,000,000	**milion** *meel·yohn*

Ordinal Numbers

first	**pierwszy** *pyehr·vshyh*
second	**drugi** *droo·gee*
third	**trzeci** *tsheh·ch'ee*
fourth	**czwarty** *chfahr·tyh*
fifth	**piąty** *pyohn·tyh*

once	**raz** *rahs*
twice	**dwa razy** *dvah rah·zyh*
three times	**trzy razy** *tshyh rah·zyh*

In Polish, as in the majority of European countries, a comma is used in place of a decimal point, and gaps are used in long numbers in place of commas. Example: 1 234 567,89 **jeden milion, dwieście trzydzieści cztery tysiące, pięćset sześćdziesiąt siedem, osiemdziesiąt dziewięć.**

Time

ESSENTIAL

What time is it?	**Czy może mi pan powiedzieć, która godzina?** *chyh moh·zheh mee pahn poh·vyeh·dj'yehch' ktoo·rah goh·dj'ee·nah*
five after [past] five	**pięć po piątej** *pyehn'ch' poh pyohn·tehy*
quarter to nine	**za piętnaście dziewiąta** *zah pyeht·nahsh'·ch'yeh dj'yeh·vyohn·tah*
ten to seven	**za dziesięć siódma** *zah dj'yeh·sh'yehn'ch' sh'yood·mah*
5:30 a.m./p.m.	**piąta trzydzieści rano/siedemnasta trzydzieści** *pyohn·tah tshyh·dj'yehsh'·ch'ee rah·noh/ sh'yeh·dehm·nahs·tah tshyh·dj'yehsh'·ch'ee*
It's noon [midday].	**Jest południe.** *yehst poh·wood·n'yeh*
It's midnight.	**Jest północ.** *yehst poow·nohts*

In Poland, time is expressed using the 24-hour clock. However, in ordinary conversation, time is usually expressed using numbers 1 to 12 with the addition of **rano** (morning), **po południu** (afternoon) or **wieczorem** (evening).

Days

ESSENTIAL

Monday	**poniedziałek**	_poh·n'yeh·dj'yah'·wehk_
Tuesday	**wtorek**	_ftoh·rehk_
Wednesday	**środa**	_sh'roh·dah_
Thursday	**czwartek**	_chfahr·tehk_
Friday	**piątek**	_pyohn·tehk_
Saturday	**sobota**	_soh·boh·tah_
Sunday	**niedziela**	_n'yeh·dj'yeh·lah_

Dates

yesterday	**wczoraj**	_fchoh·rahy_
today	**dzisiaj**	_dj'ee·sh'yahy_
tomorrow	**jutro**	_yoot·roh_
day	**dzień**	_dj'yehn'_
week	**tydzień**	_tyh·dj'yehn'_
month	**miesiąc**	_myeh·sh'ohnts_
year	**rok**	_rohk_

Months

January	**styczeń**	_styh·chehn'_
February	**luty**	_loo·tyh_

March	**marzec** _mah_•zhehts
April	**kwiecień** _kfyeh_•ch'yehn'
May	**maj** mahy
June	**czerwiec** _chehr_•vyehts
July	**lipiec** _lee_•pyehts
August	**sierpień** _sh'yehr_•pyehn'
September	**wrzesień** _vzheh_•sh'yehn'
October	**październik** pahzh'•_dj'yehr_•n'eek
November	**listopad** lees•_toh_•paht
December	**grudzień** _groo_•dj'yehn'

Seasons

spring	**wiosna** _vyohs_•nah
summer	**lato** _lah_•toh
fall [autumn]	**jesień** _yeh_•sh'yehn'
winter	**zima** _zh'ee_•mah

Holidays

January 1	**Nowy Rok** New Year's Day
January 6	**Trzech Króli** Epiphany
March/April (moveable)	**Wielkanoc** Easter
May 1	**Święto 1 Maja** Labor Day
May 3	**Konstytucja 3 Maja** Constitution Day
Thursday in May/June (moveable)	**Boże Ciało** Corpus Christi
August 15	**Wniebowzięcie** Assumption Day
November 1	**Wszystkich Świętych** All Saints' Day
November 11	**Święto Niepodległości** Independence Day
December 25 & 26	**Boże Narodzenie** Christmas

Conversion Tables

When you know	Multiply by	To find
ounces	*28.3*	grams
pounds	*0.45*	kilograms
inches	*2.54*	centimeters
feet	*0.3*	meters
miles	*1.61*	kilometers
square inches	*6.45*	sq. centimeters
square feet	*0.09*	sq. meters
square miles	*2.59*	sq. kilometers
pints (U.S./Brit)	*0.47/0.56*	liters
gallons (U.S./Brit)	*3.8/4.5*	liters
Fahrenheit	*5/9, after 32*	Centigrade
Centigrade	*9/5, then +32*	Fahrenheit

Kilometers to Miles Conversions

1 km	0.62 miles
5 km	3.1 miles
10 km	6.2 miles
50 km	31 miles
100 km	62 miles

Measurement

1 gram	**gram** *grahm*	= 0.035 oz.
1 kilogram (kg)	**kilo** *kee·loh*	= 2.2 lb
1 liter (l)	**litr** *leetre*	= 1.06 U.S./ 0.88 Brit. quarts
1 centimeter (cm)	**centymetr** *tsehn·tyh·mehtr*	= 0.4 inch
1 meter (m)	**metr** *mehtr*	= 3.28 feet
1 kilometer (km)	**kilometr** *kee·loh·mehtr*	= 0.62 mile

Temperature

-40°C – -40°F	**-1°C** – 30°F	**20°C** – 68°F
-30°C – -22°F	**0°C** – 32°F	**25°C** – 77°F
-20°C – -4°F	**5°C** – 41°F	**30°C** – 86°F
-10°C – 14°F	**10°C** – 50°F	**35°C** – 95°F
-5°C – 23°F	**15°C** – 59°F	

Oven Temperature

100°C – 212°F	**177°C** – 350°F
121°C – 250°F	**204°C** – 400°F
149°C – 300°F	**260°C** – 500°F

Dictionary

A

a little trochę
a lot dużo
a.m. przed południem
accept *v* zaakceptować
accident (road) wypadek
accidentally przypadkowo
across przez
acrylic *adj* akrylowy; *n* akryl
actor aktor
adapter przejściówka
address adres
admission charge opłata za wstęp
adult *n* dorosły
afraid przestraszony
after (time) po; **(place)** za
afternoon popołudnie
aftershave płyn po goleniu
ago temu
agree zgadzać się
air conditioner klimatyzator
air conditioning klimatyzacja
air mattress materac nadmuchiwany

air pump kompresor
airline linia lotnicza
airmail poczta lotnicza
airport lotnisko
air-sickness bag torebka na chorobę lotniczą
aisle seat miejsce przy przejściu
alarm clock budzik
allergic uczulony
allergy uczulenie
allowance ilość
almost prawie
alone sam
already już
also również
alter poprawić
aluminum foil folia aluminiowa
always zawsze
amazing zdumiewający
ambassador ambasador
ambulance karetka
American *adj* amerykański; *n* Amerykanin
amount (money) kwota
and i

| **adj** adjective | **BE** British English | **prep** preposition |
| **adv** adverb | **n** noun | **v** verb |

anesthetia znieczulenie
animal zwierzę
another inny
antacid środek neutralizujący kwas
antibiotics antybiotyk
antique *n* antyk
antiseptic aseptyczny
antiseptic cream krem aseptyczny
any jakiś
anyone ktoś
apartment mieszkanie
apologize przepraszać
appendix wyrostek robaczkowy
appetite apetyt
appetizer przekąska
appointment (business) spotkanie;
  (doctor) wizyta
approximately około
arcade salon gier
area code numer kierunkowy
arm (body part) ramię
around (time) około; **(place)** po
arrive (car, train) przyjeżdżać;
  (plane) lądować
art gallery galeria sztuki
artist artysta
ashtray popielniczka
ask (question) pytać; **(request)**
  prosić
aspirin aspiryna
asthma astma

at (time) o; **(place)** na
ATM bankomat
attack atak
attractive atrakcyjny
audioguide przewodnik
  dźwiękowy
Australia Australia
authenticity autentyczność
automatic trasmission
  automatycza skrzynia biegów
autumn [BE] jesień
available (free) wolne
avalanche lawina

B

baby dziecko
baby food jedzenie dla dzieci
baby wipe wilgotne chusteczki
  pielęgnacyjne
babysitter opiekunka
back (head) tył; **(body)** grzbiet
backache ból grzbietu
backpack *n* plecak; *v* wędrować z
  plecakiem
bad zły
bag torba
baggage [BE] bagaż
baggage room przechowalnia
  bagażu
bakery piekarnia
balcony balkon

ball piłka
ballet balet
band (music) zespół
bandage bandaż
bank bank
bar bar
barber fryzjer męski
basement piwnica
basketball koszykówka
bath n wanna; v kąpiel
bathroom łazienka
battery bateria; **(car)** akumulator
battle site pole bitwy
be być
beach plaża
beautiful piękny
because ponieważ
bed łóżko
bedding pościel
bedroom sypialnia
before (time) przed
begin zaczynać
beginner początkujący
behind za
belong należeć
belt pasek
berth (ship) koja; **(train)** kuszetka
best najlepszy
better lepszy
between pomiędzy
bib śliniaczek

bicycle rower
bicycle route szlak rowerowy
big duży
bikini bikini
bill (restaurant) rachunek
binoculars lornetka
bird ptak
birthday urodziny
bite n ugryzienie
bitter gorzki
bizarre dziwaczny
black czarny
bladder pęcherz moczowy
bland mdły
blanket koc
bleach wybielacz
bleed krwawić
bleeding krwotok
blister pęcherz
block v blokować
blood krew
blood pressure ciśnienie krwi
blouse bluzka
blow-dry suszenie z modelowaniem
blue niebieski
board pokład
boarding card karta pokładowa
boat trip przejażdżka statkiem
boil v gotować
boiler boiler

bone kość
book książka
bookstore księgarnia
boots botki
boring nudny
born *v* urodzić się
borrow pożyczyć
botanical garden ogród botaniczny
bottle butelka
bottle opener otwieracz do butelek
bowl miska
box (container) pudełko
boy chłopiec
boyfriend chłopak
bra biustonosz
bracelet bransoletka
brake hamulec
break (destroy) zepsuć; **(body part)** złamać
break down (go wrong) zepsuć się
breakfast śniadanie
breast (body) pierś
breathe oddychać
bridge most
briefs (clothing) majtki
bring przenieść
Britain Wielka Brytania
British *adj* brytyjski; *n* Brytyjczyk
brochure broszura

broken zepsuty
bronchitis bronchit
brooch broszka
brother brat
browse patrzeć
bruise siniak
bucket wiaderko
bug robak
build budować
building budynek
bulletin board tablica informacyjna
burn *n* oparzenie
bus autobus
bus route trasa autobusowa
bus station dworzec autobusowy
bus stop przystanek autobusowy
business biznes
business class klasa biznes
busy zajęty
but ale
butane gas butan
butcher (store) rzeźnik
button guzik
buy kupić

C

cabaret kabaret
café kawiarnia
call (ambulance) wezwać; **(telephone)** zadzwonić

camera aparat fotograficzny
camera case futerał na aparat
camp *n* obóz; *v* obozować
campfire ognisko
campsite pole namiotowe
can *n* puszka; *v* móc
can opener otwieracz do puszek
Canada Kanada
canal kanał
cancel odwołać
cancer rak
cap (dental) koronka; **(clothing)** czapka
car samochód; **(train)** wagon
car hire [BE] wynajem samochodów
car insurance ubezpiecznie samochodowe
car park parking
car rental wynajem samochodów
car seat fotelik dziecięcy
carafe karafka
card karta
careful ostrożny
carpet dywan
carry-on (luggage) bagaż podręczny
cart wózek
carton karton
cash (money) gotówka; *v* zrealizować

cashier kasjer
casino kasyno
castle zamek
catch (bus) złapać
cathedral katedra
cave jaskinia
CD płyta
CD player odtwarzacz płyt kompaktowych
cell phone telefon komórkowy
cemetery cmentarz
ceramics ceramika
certificate certyfikat
chain łańcuszek
change *n* **(small coins)** drobne; **(in shop)** reszta; *v* **(bus, train)** przesiadać się; **(baby)** przewinąć; **(money)** wymieniać; **(reservation)** zmienić, **(clothes)** przebrać się
changing room przebieralnia
charcoal węgiel drzewny
charge opłata
cheap tani
check *n* czek
check in *n* odprawa
check out (hotel) wyrejestrować się
checkbook książeczka czekowa
check-in desk stanowisko odprawy

chemical toilet chemiczna toaleta
chemist [BE] apteka
cheque [BE] czek
chess szachy
chest (body) klatka persiowa
child dziecko
child's cot łóżeczko dziecięce
child's seat krzesełko dla dziecka
church kościół
cigar cygaro
cigarette papieros
clamp założyć blokadę na koła
clean *adj* czysty; *v* wyczyścić
cliff klif
cling film [BE] folia do żywności
clinic klinika
clock zegar
close (near) niedaleko; **(store)** zamykać
clothing store sklep odzieżowy
cloudy pochmurno
coach [BE] **(long-distance bus)** autokar
coat płaszcz
coat check szatnia
coat hanger wieszak
cockroach karaluch
coin moneta
cold *adj* zimny; *adv* zimno; *n* **(illness)** przeziębienie

collapse upaść
collect zebrać
collect call rozmowa na koszt rozmówcy
color kolor
color film film kolorowy
comb grzebień
come przyjść
come back (return) wrócić
commission prowizja
company (companionship) towarzystwo; **(business)** firma
compartment (train) przedział
composer kompozytor
computer komputer
concert koncert
concert hall sala koncertowa
concession koncesja
concussion wstrząs mózgu
conditioner odżywka
condom prezerwatywa
conductor dyrygent
confirm potwierdzić
confirmation potwierdzenie
connect (internet) połączyć się z siecią
connection (train) połączenie
conscious (awake) przytomny
constant ciągły
constipation zaparcie
consulate konsulat

consult skonsultować się
contact skontaktować się
contact lens szkło kontaktowe
contagious zakaźny
contain zawierać
contraceptive środek antykoncepcyjny
convenience store sklep osiedlowy
cook v gotować; n kucharz
cooker [BE] kuchenka
cooking (cuisine) kuchnia
cooking facilities możliwość gotowania
copper miedź
copy kopia
corkscrew korkociąg
correct prawidłowy
cosmetics kosmetyki
cost v kosztować
cot rozkładane łóżko
cottage domek
cotton (material) bawełna
cough n kaszel; v kaszleć
country kraj
country code numer kierunkowy
country music muzyka country
course (meal) danie; **(path)** droga
cousin kuzyn
cramp skurcz
credit card karta kredytowa

credit card number numer karty kredytowej
crib łóżeczko dziecięce
cross v przejść
cross-country skis biegówki
crowd tłok
crowded zatłoczony
crown (dental) koronka; **(royal)** korona
cruise n rejs
crystal (quartz) kryształ
cup filiżanka
cupboard szafka kuchenna
currency waluta
currency exchange office kantor
currency exchange rate kurs wymiany
curtain zasłona
customs urząd celny
customs declaration deklaracja celna
cut (hair) strzyżenie; **(wound)** rana cięta
cut glass cięte szkło
cutlery sztućce
cycling kolarstwo

D

daily adj codzienny; adv codziennie
damaged zniszczony

damp *adj* wilgotny
dance *n* taniec; *v* tańczyć
dance club dyskoteka
dangerous niebezpieczny
dark ciemny
daughter córka
dawn świt
day dzień
day charge opłata za dzień
day ticket bilet jednodniowy
day trip wycieczka jednodniowa
dead (battery) wyczerpany
deaf głuchy
deck chair leżak
declare zadeklarować
deduct odejmować
deep głęboki
defrost rozmrozić
degree (temperature) stopień
delay opóźnienie
delayed opóźniony
delicatessen delikatesy
delicious smaczny
deliver dostarczyć
delivery dostawa
denim drelich
dental floss nić dentystyczna
dentist dentysta
denture proteza dentystyczna
deodorant dezodorant
depart (train, bus) odjeżdżać;

(plane) startować
department store dom towarowy
departure lounge poczekalnia
departures (airport) hala odlotów
deposit (security) kaucja
describe opisać
description opis
destination (travel) cel podróży
detail szczegół
detergent środek czystości
develop (photos) wywołać
diabetes cukrzyca
diabetic *n* cukrzyk
dialing code numer kierunkowy
diamond brylant
diaper pieluszka
diarrhea biegunka
dice kostka do gry
dictionary słownik
diesel diesel
diet dieta
difficult trudny
dining car wagon restauracyjny
dining room jadalnia
dinner kolacja
direct *adj* **(train, journey)**
    bezpośredni; *v* **(to a place)**
    wskazać kierunek
direction kierunek
director (company) dyrektor
directory (telephone) książka

telefoniczna
dirty brudny
disabled *n* niepełnosprawny
discount zniżka
discount card karta rabatowa
dish (meal) danie
dishcloth ścierka
dishwasher zmywarka
dishwashing liquid płyn do
  zmywania
display cabinet gablota
display case gablota
disposable camera aparat
  jednorazowy
disturb przeszkadzać
dive (scuba dive) nurkować; **(jump)**
  skakać
diving equipment sprzęt do
  nurkowania
divorced rozwiedziony
dizziness zawroty głowy
do robić
doctor lekarz
doll lalka
dollar dolar
domestic (flight) krajowy
door drzwi
double bed podwójne łóżko
double room pokój dwuosobowy
downtown area centrum
dozen tuzin

dress sukienka
drink *n* **(alcoholic)** drink; *v* pić
drink menu lista drinków
drip ciec
drive jechać
driver (car) kierowca
driver's license prawo jazdy
drown tonąć
drugstore drogeria
drunk pijany
dry cleaner's pralnia chemiczna
dry-clean czyścić **(chemicznie)**
dubbed dubbingowany
dummy [BE] smoczek
during podczas
dustbin [BE] śmietnik
duty cło
duvet kołdra

E

ear ucho
ear drops krople do uszu
earache ból ucha
early *adj* wczesny; *adv* wcześnie
earring kolczyk
east wschód
easy łatwy
eat jeść
economy class klasa turystyczna
elastic *adj* elastyczny
electric shaver golarka elektryczna

electrical outlet gniazdko elektryczne
electronic elektroniczny
elevator winda
e-mail *n* e-mail; *v* napisać maila
e-mail address adres e-mail
embassy ambasada
embroidery haft
emerald szmaragd
emergency nagły wypadek
emergency exit wyjście awaryjne
emergency ward izba przyjęć
empty pusty
enamel emalia
end *n* koniec; *v* kończyć (się)
engaged zaręczony
engine silnik
engineer inżynier
England Anglia
English *adj* angielski; *n* Anglik
enjoy podobać się
enjoyable przyjemny
enlarge (photos) powiększyć
enough dość
entertainment guide program rozrywek
entrance fee opłata za wstęp
envelope koperta
epilepsy epilepsja
epileptic *n* epileptyk
equipment (sports) sprzęt

era epoka
error błąd
escalator schody ruchome
escape route droga ewakuacyjna
essential niezbędny
e-ticket bilet elektroniczny
eurocheque euroczek
European Union Unia Europejska
evening wieczór
evening dress strój wieczorowy
every każdy
examination (medical) badanie
example przykład
except oprócz
excess baggage nadbagaż
exchange wymienić
exchange rate kurs wymiany
excursion wycieczka
exhausted wyczerpany
exit wyjście
expensive drogi
experienced zaawansowany
expiration date data ważności
expiry date [BE] data ważności
exposure (photos) naświetlanie
express ekspres
express mail priorytet
extension (phone) wewnętrzny
extra (additional) dodatkowy
extract (tooth) wyrwać
eye oko

F

fabric materiał
face twarz
facial zabieg oczyszczania skóry
faint v zemdleć
fairground wesołe miasteczko
fall n jesień
family rodzina
famous sławny
fan (electric) wentylator
far daleko
farm gospodarstwo
far-sighted dalekowidz
fast szybko
father ojciec
faucet kran
faulty wadliwy
favorite ulubiony
fax faks
fee opłata
feed nakarmić
feel czuć (się)
female kobieta
ferry prom
fever gorączka
few parę
fiancé narzeczony
fiancée narzeczona
field pole
fight (brawl) bójka
fill out (a form) wypełnić

fill up (car) nalać do pełna
filling (dental) plomba
film (camera, movie) film
filter filtr
find znaleźć
fine (well) dobrze; **(penalty)** grzywna
finger palec
fire pożar
fire alarm alarm pożarowy
fire brigade [BE] straż pożarna
fire department straż pożarna
fire door drzwi przeciwpożarowe
fire escape schody pożarowe
fire exit wyjście awaryjne
fire extinguisher gaśnica
first class pierwsza klasa
first floor parter
fish store sklep rybny
fit v pasować
fitting room przymierzalnia
fix v naprawić
flame płomień
flashlight latarka
flat (tire) przebity
flavor smak
flea pchła
flea market pchli targ
flight lot
flight number numer lotu
floor (level) piętro

florist kwiaciarnia
flower kwiat
flu grypa
flush (toilet) spuszczać wodę
fly n mucha; v latać
fog mgła
folk art sztuka ludowa
folk music muzyka ludowa
follow (pursue) podążać; **(road, sign)** jechać zgodnie z
food jedzenie
food poisoning zatrucie pokarmowe
foot stopa
football [BE] piłka nożna
footpath [BE] dróżka
for (time) przez; **(duration)** na
foreign currency obca waluta
forest las
forget zapominać
fork widelec
form formularz
formal dress strój formalny
fortunately na szczęście
fountain fontanna
foyer (hotel, theater) foyer
fracture złamanie
frame (glasses) oprawka
free (available) wolny; **(without charge)** bezpłatny
freezer zamrażarka
frequently często

fresh świeży
friend przyjaciel
friendly (person) przyjazny; **(place, atmosphere)** przyjemny
frightened przerażony
from (place) z; **(time)** od
front przód
frost mróz
frying pan patelnia
fuel paliwo
full pełny
full board z pełnym wyżywieniem
fun zabawa
funny śmieszny
furniture meble

G

gallon galon
game gra; **(sports)** mecz
garage (mechanic) warsztat samochodowy; **(parking lot)** garaż
garbage śmieci
garbage bag worek na śmieci
garden ogródek
gas (fuel) benzyna
gas station stacja benzynowa
gate (airport) wyjście
gauze gaza
genuine prawdziwy
get (buy) kupić; **(find)** znaleźć
get back (return) wrócić

get off (bus/train) wysiąść
get to dojechać do
gift prezent
gift shop sklep z upominkami
giftwrap zapakować na prezent
girl dziewczyna
girlfriend dziewczyna
give dać
glass (non-alcoholic) szklanka; **(alcoholic)** kieliszek
glasses (optical) okulary
glove rękawiczka
go (on foot) iść; **(by bus, train)** jechać; **(by plane)** lecieć
go away odejść
goggles (swimming) okularki; **(skiing)** gogle
gold złoto
golf golf
golf club kij golfowy
golf course pole golfowe
good dobry
good evening dobry wieczór
good morning dzień dobry
good night dobranoc
goodbye do widzenia
gram gram
grandfather dziadek
grandmother babcia
grandparents dziadkowie
grass trawa

gray szary
great *adj* świetny; *adv* świetnie
green zielony
greengrocer [BE] warzywniak
grocery store sklep spożywczy
ground (earth) ziemia
ground floor [BE] parter
groundcloth podłoga namiotu
groundsheet [BE] podłoga namiotu
group grupa
group guide przewodnik grupowy
group leader kierownik grupy
group ticket bilet grupowy
guarantee gwarancja
guest gość
guesthouse pensjonat
guide (tour) przewodnik
guidebook przewodnik
guided tour wycieczka z przewodnikiem
guided walk wycieczka piesza z przewodnikiem
guitar gitara
gym siłownia
gynecologist ginekolog

H

hair włosy
hair gel żel do włosów
haircut strzyżenie włosów

hairdresser fryzjer
hairspray lakier do włosów
half pół
hammer młotek
hand ręka
hand luggage [BE] bagaż
  podręczny
hand washable prać ręcznie
handbag torebka
handicapped niepełnosprawny
handicrafts wyroby rękodzielnicze
handkerchief chusteczka
hanger wieszak
hangover n kac
happy szczęśliwy
harbor port
hard (texture) twardy; **(difficult)**
  ciężki
hat kapelusz
have mieć
hay fever katar sienny
head n głowa; v **(go towards)**
  jechać w kierunku
head waiter kierownik sali
headache ból głowy
health zdrowie
health food store sklep ze
  zdrową żywnością
health insurance ubezpieczenie
  zdrowotne
hear słyszeć

hearing aid aparat słuchowy
heart serce; **(cards)** kier
heart attack zawał serca
heat ogrzewanie
heater grzejnik
heating [BE] ogrzewanie
heavy ciężki
height wzrost
helmet kask
help pomoc
hemorrhoids hemoroidy
her jej
here tutaj
hernia przepuklina
herpes opryszczka
hers jej
high wysoki
highchair wysokie krzesełko
highlight v **(hair)** robić pasemka;
  (stress) podkreślić
highway autostrada
hiking (general) turystyka
  piesza; **(trip)** wędrówka
hill wzgórze
him niego
hire [BE] v wynająć
his jego
historic site miejsce historyczne
hobby (pastime) hobby
holiday [BE] wakacje
holiday resort miejscowość

wypoczynkowa
home (be/go) w domu/do domu
honeymoon miesiąc miodowy
horse koń
horse racing wyścigi konne
hospital szpital
hot gorący
hot spring gorące źródło
hotel hotel
hour godzina
house dom
housewife gospodyni domowa
hundred sto
hungry głodny
hurt boleć
husband mąż

I

ice-cream parlor lodziarnia
icy oblodzony
identification dowód tożsamości
ill chory
illegal nielegalny
imitation imitacja
in (place) w; **(period of time)** w ciągu
included wliczony
incredible niewiarygodny
indicate wskazywać
indigestion niestrawność
indoor pool kryty basen

inexpensive niedrogi
infected zakażony
infection infekcja
inflammation zapalenie
informal (dress) nieformalny
information (desk, office) infomacja
injection zastrzyk
injured ranny
innocent niewinny
insect insekt
insect bite ugryzienie owada
insect repellent środek na owady
insect sting użądlenie
inside w środku
insist nalegać
insomnia bezsenność
instead zamiast
instruction instrukcja
instructor instruktor
insulin insulina
insurance ubezpieczenie
insurance card polisa ubezpieczeniowa
insurance certificate [BE] polisa ubezpieczeniowa
insurance claim wniosek o odszkodowanie
interest (hobby) zainteresowanie
interested zainteresowany
interesting interesujący

international (flight)
  międzynarodowy
International Student Card
  Międzynarodowa Karta Studenta
internet internet
internet cafe kafejka internetowa
interpreter tłumacz ustny
intersection skrzyżowanie
into do
intolerance nietolerancja
invite zaprosić
iodine jodyna
Ireland Irlandia
iron *n* żelazko; *v* prasować
itch swędzieć
item (object) przedmiot
itemized bill szczegółowy
  rachunek

J

jacket (men's) marynarka;
  (women's) żakiet
jaw szczęka
jazz jazz
jeans dżinsy
jellyfish meduza
jet-ski skuter wodny
jeweler jubiler
jewelry biżuteria
join (a group) dołączyć się
joint (body) staw

joke żart
journalist dziennikarz
journey podróż
jug (water) dzbanek
jumper [BE] pulower
junction [BE] (intersection)
  skrzyżowanie

K

keep zatrzymać
kerosene nafta
kettle czajnik
key klucz
key card (hotel) karta
kiddie pool brodzik
kidney nerka
kilometer kilometr
kind *adj* uprzejmy; *n* rodzaj
kiss *n* pocałunek; *v* całować
kitchen kuchnia
kitchen foil [BE] folia aluminiowa
knee kolano
knickers [BE] majtki
knife nóż
know wiedzieć
kosher koszerny

L

label (sticker) nalepka; **(on**
  bottle) etykieta
lace koronka

ladder drabina
lake jezioro
lamp lampa
land *v* lądować
language course kurs językowy
large (size) duży
last *adj* ostatni; **(previous)** zeszły;
  v trwać
late (not early) późny; **(delayed)**
  opóźniony
later później
laundromat pralnia
  samoobsługowa
laundry facilities pralnia
lawyer prawnik
laxative środek przeczyszczający
lead *n* smycz; *v* prowadzić
leader (ideological) przywódca;
  (manager) menedżer
leak *n* przeciek; *v* **(roof, pipe)**
  przeciekać
learn (language) uczyć się
leather skóra
leave (depart) odjeżdżać;
  (deposit) zostawić; **(on foot)**
  odejść; **(depart of plane)**
  odlatywać
left *adj* lewy
left-luggage office [BE]
  przechowalnia bagażu
leg noga

legal legalny
lend pożyczyć
lens (optical) soczewka;
  (camera) obiektyw
lense cap nakładka na obiektyw
less mniej
lesson lekcja
let *v* **(permit)** pozwolić
let go puścić
letter list
library biblioteka
license plate number numer
  rejestracyjny
life preserver koło ratunkowe
lifeboat łódź ratunkowa
lifeguard ratownik
lifejacket kamizelka ratunkowa
lift [BE] winda
lift pass (skiing) skipass
light *adj* **(weight)** lekki; **(color)**
  jasny; *n* światło
light bulb żarówka
lighter *adj* jaśniejszy; *n*
  zapalniczka
like *v* lubić
limousine limuzyna
line (metro) linia metra
linen len
lip warga
lipgloss błyszczyk
lipstick szminka**

liquor store sklep monopolowy
liter litr
little (small) mały
live mieszkać
liver wątroba
living room salon
lobby (theater) foyer; **(hotel)** hol
local lokalny
lock n **(door)** zamek; **(bike)** blokada; v zamknąć
log off wylogować się
log on zalogować się
login login
long długi
long-distance bus autokar
long-sighted [BE] dalekowidz
loose luźny
lorry [BE] ciężarówka
lose (item) zgubić; **(person)** stracić
lost-and-found biuro rzeczy znalezionych
lost-property office [BE] biuro rzeczy znalezionych
love n miłość; v kochać
lovely śliczny
low niski
lower (berth) dolny
low-fat o niskiej zawartości tłuszczu
luck szczęście

luggage bagaż
luggage cart wózek na bagaż
luggage locker schowek na baga<
luggage trolley [BE] wózek na bagaż
lump guz
lunch obiad
lung płuco

M

machine washable prać w pralce
madam pani
magazine czasopismo
magnificent wspaniały
maid pokojówka
mail n poczta; v wysłać
mailbox skrzynka pocztowa
main główny
make zrobić
male mężczyzna
mallet młotek drewniany
manager menadżer
manicure manicure
many dużo
map mapa
market (job market) rynek; **(place to buy)** targ
married żonaty
mascara tusz do rzęs
mask (diving) maska
mass msza

massage masaż
match (game) mecz; **(light)** zapałka
mattress materac
maybe może
me ja
meal posiłek
measles odra
measure zmierzyć
measurement miara
measuring cup miarka kuchenna
measuring spoon łyżka do odmierzania
mechanic mechanik
medication lek
medicine lekarstwo
medium średni
meet (get to know) poznać; **(appointment)** spotkać
meeting place miejsce zbiórki
meeting point [BE] miejsce zbiórki
member (association) członek
memorial (war) pomnik
mention wspominać
menu menu
message wiadomość
metal metal
metro map mapa metra
metro station stacja metra
microwave (oven) kuchenka mikrofalowa
midday [BE] południe
midnight północ
migraine migrena
million milion
mine mój
mini-bar mini-bar
minute (time) minuta
mirror lustro
miss (lack) brakować; **(lost)** zaginąć
mistake błąd
misunderstanding nieporozumienie
mobile home przyczepa mieszkalna
mobile phone [BE] telefon komórkowy
moisturizer (cream) krem nawilżający
monastery klasztor
money pieniądze
money order przekaz pieniężny
month miesiąc
monument pomnik
mop mop
moped motorower
more więcej
morning rano
mosque meczet
mosquito bite ukąszenie komara

mother matka
motion sickness choroba lokomocyjna
motorbike motor
motorboat motorówka
motorcycle motor
motorway [BE] autostrada
mountain góra
mountain bike rower górski
mountain pass przełęcz górska
mountain range łańcuch górski
moustache wąsy
mouth usta
move ruszać
movie film
movie theater kino
much dużo
mug n kubek; v napadać
mugging napad
mumps świnka
muscle mięsień
museum muzeum
music muzyka
music store sklep muzyczny
musician muzyk
must v musieć
my mój

N

name imię
napkin serwetka

nappy [BE] pieluszka
narrow wąski
national narodowy
national park park narodowy
nationality obywatelstwo
native tutejszy
nature reserve rezerwat przyrody
nature trail szlak przyrodniczy
nausea mdłości
near niedaleko
nearby niedaleko
near-sighted krótkowidz
necessary konieczny
neck (body) szyja
necklace naszyjnik
need v potrzebować
nerve nerw
nervous system układ nerwowy
never nigdy
new nowy
newsagent [BE] kiosk z gazetami
newspaper gazeta
newsstand kiosk z gazetami
next następny
nice miły
night noc
night club klub nocny
no nie
noisy hałaśliwy
none żaden
nonsense bzdura

non-smoking *adj* dla niepalących
noon południe
normal normalny
north północ
nose nos
nothing nic
notify zawiadomić
now teraz
number numer
nurse pielęgniarka
nylon nylon

O

occasionally czasami
occupied zajęty
office (place) biuro
off-licence [BE] sklep
  monopolowy
often często
okay okay
old stary
old town stare miasto
on (day, date) w
once raz
one jeden
one-way w jedną stonę
one-way ticket bilet w jedną
  stronę
open *adj* otwarty; *v* otwierać
opening hours godziny otwarcia
opera opera

opera house opera
operation operacja
opposite naprzeciwko
optician optyk
or albo
orange (color) pomarańczowy
order *n* zamówienie; *v* zamówić
our(s) nasz
outdoor pool basen otwarty
outrageous (price) horrendalny
outside na zewnątrz
oval owalny
oven piekarnik
overcharge *v* policzyć za dużo
overheat przegrzać się
overnight na noc
owe być dłużnym
own *adj* własny
owner właściciel

P

p.m. po południu
pacifier smoczek
pack pakować
package przesyłka
paddling pool [BE] brodzik
padlock kłódka
pail (toy) wiaderko
pain ból
painkiller środek przeciwbólowy
paint *v* malować

painter malarz
painting obraz
pair para
palace pałac
panorama panorama
pants spodnie
pantyhose rajstopy
paper napkin serwetka papierowa
paper towel ręcznik papierowy
paracetamol [BE] paracetamol
paralysis paraliż
parcel [BE] paczka
parent rodzic
park n park; v parkować
parking garage parking
   podziemny
parking lot parking
parking meter parkometr
parliament building budynek
   parlamentu
partner partner
party (social) przyjęcie
passenger pasażer
passport paszport
passport number numer
   paszportu
password hasło
pastry shop sklep cukierniczy
patch załatać
patient n pacjent
pavement [BE] chodnik

pay płacić
pay phone automat telefoniczny
payment zapłata
peak szczyt
pearl perła
pedestrian pieszy
pedestrian crossing przejście dla
   pieszych
pedestrian zone strefa zamknięta
   dla ruchu kołowego
peg [BE] spinacz do bielizny
pen długopis
per za
perhaps być może
period (time) okres; **(menstrual)**
   miesiączka
person osoba
petrol [BE] benzyna
petrol station [BE] stacja
   benzynowa
pewter cyna
pharmacy apteka
phone n telefon; v dzwonić
phone card karta telefoniczna
photo zdjęcie
photocopier kopiarka
photograph zdjęcie
photographer fotograf
phrase zwrot
phrase book rozmówki
pick up odebrać

picnic piknik
picnic area miejsce piknikowe
piece (item) sztuka; **(amount)** kawałek
pill (contraceptive) pigułka antykoncepcyjna; **(tablet)** tabletka
pillow poduszka
pillow case poszewka na poduszkę
pink różowy
pipe (smoking) fajka
pitch (camping) pole namiotowe
pizzeria pizzeria
place miejsce
plan *n* plan; *v* planować
plane samolot
plant (greenery) roślina
plaster [BE] plaster
plastic *adj* plastikowy
plastic bag torebka plastikowa
plastic wrap folia spożywcza
plate talerz
platform peron; **[BE]** tor
platinum platyna
play *n* **(theater)** sztuka; *v* grać
playground plac zabaw
playing field boisko
pleasant przyjemny
please proszę
plug zatyczka
plunger przepychacz
pneumonia zapalenie płuc

point wskazać
poison trucizna
Poland Polska
police policja
police report raport policyjny
police station komisariat policji
Polish *adj* polski; *n* Polak
pollen count stężenie pyłków w powietrzu
polyester poliester
pond staw
pop (music) pop
popular popularny; **(well-known)** znany
port (harbor) port
porter bagażowy
portion porcja
possible możliwy
post [BE] *n* **(mail)** poczta; *v* wysłać
post office poczta
postage opłata
postcard pocztówka
poster plakat
pot (for cooking) garnek; **(for tea)** dzbanek
pottery ceramika
pound (sterling) funt
powdery (snow) puszysty
power (electricity) prąd
precipice przepaść

pregnant w ciąży
prescribe przepisać
prescription recepta
present (gift) prezent
press naciskać
pretty ładny
price cena
print n sztych; v drukować
prison więzienie
produce store sklep spożywczy
profession zawód
program program
pronounce wymawiać
pub pub
public n publiczność; adj publiczny
pump (gas station) pompa
puncture przebicie
pure czysty
purple fioletowy
purse torebka
push-chair [BE] wózek spacerowy
put włożyć

Q

quality jakość
quarter ćwierć; (time) kwadrans
queue [BE] n kolejka; v stać w kolejce
quick szybki
quickly szybko
quiet cichy

R

race course [BE] tor wyścigowy
racetrack tor wyścigowy
racket (tennis, squash) rakieta
railway station [BE] stacja kolejowa
rain n deszcz
raincoat płaszcz przeciwdeszczowy
rape n gwałt; v zgwałcić
rapids progi rzeczne
rare (unusual) rzadki
rash wysypka
razor maszynka do golenia
razor blade żyletka
read v czytać
ready gotowy
real (genuine) prawdziwy
rear tylny
receipt paragon
receive odebrać
reception (desk) recepcja
receptionist recepcjonista
recommend polecić
red czerwony
reduction (price) obniżka
refrigerator lodówka
refund zwrot pieniędzy
region (area) region
registered mail list polecony
registration form formularz rejestracji
reliable niezawodny

religion religia
remember pamiętać
rent wynająć
rental car wynajęty samochód
repair *n* naprawa; *v* naprawić
repeat powtórzyć
replacement wymiana
replacement part część zamienna
report (crime) zgłosić
require wymagać
reservation rezerwacja
reservations desk okienko rezerwacji
reserve *v* rezerwować
rest *v* odpoczywać
restaurant restauracja
restroom toaleta
return wrócić; **(surrender)** zwrócić
return ticket [BE] bilet powrotny
reverse-charge call [BE] rozmowa na koszt rozmówcy
rheumatism reumatyzm
rib żebro
right (correct) poprawny; **(good)** dobry
right of way pierwszeństwo przejazdu
ring pierścionek
river rzeka
road droga
road map mapa drogowa

road sign znak drogowy
rob obrabować
robbery rabunek
rock (music) rock; **(land formation)** skała
romantic romantyczny
roof dach
roof-rack bagażnik dachowy
room (hotel) pokój
room service room service
rope lina
round okrągły
round-trip ticket bilet powrotny
route trasa
rubbish [BE] śmieci
rude niegrzeczny
ruins ruiny

S

safe *adj* bezpieczny; *n* sejf
safety bezpieczeństwo
safety pin agrafka
sand piasek
sandal sandał
sanitary napkin podpaska
sanitary pad [BE] podpaska
satellite TV telewizja satelitarna
satin satyna
saucepan rondel
sauna sauna
say *v* powiedzieć

scarf szalik
scissors nożyczki
Scotland Szkocja
screwdriver śrubokręt
sea morze
seasickness choroba moska
season ticket bilet okresowy
seat (train) miejsce
seat reservation (train)
  miejscówka
second class druga klasa
secondhand store sklep z używaną
  odzieżą
secretary sekretarka
sedative środek uspokajający
see (spot) zobaczyć; **(inspect)**
  sprawdzić; **(observe, witness)**
  widzieć
self-employed samozatrudniony
self-service (gas station)
  samoobsługa
sell sprzedawać
send wysłać
senior citizen emeryt
separated w separacji
separately osobno
serious poważny
service (in restaurant) obsługa;
  (religious) nabożeństwo
sex seks; **(gender)** płeć
shade odcień

shady cienisty
shallow płytki
shampoo szampon
share v dzielić
sharp ostry
shaving cream krem do golenia
she ona
sheet (bed) prześcieradło
shirt (men's) koszula; **(women's)**
  bluzka
shock (electric) porażenie
shoe but
shoe repair naprawa obuwia
shoe store sklep z obuwiem
shop assistant sprzedawca
shopping area centrum handlowe
shopping basket koszyk
shopping cart wózek
shopping centre [BE] centrum
  handlowe
shopping mall centrum handlowe
shopping trolley [BE] wózek
short adj **(length)** krótki; **(person)**
  niski
shorts (clothing) szorty
short-sighted [BE] krótkowidz
shoulder bark
shovel (toy) łopatka
show n **(presentation)** pokaz;
  (theater) sztuka; v pokazać
shower prysznic

shrine kapliczka
shut v zamykać; adj zamknięty
shutter okiennica
side (head) bok
side order dodatek
side street boczna uliczka
sidewalk chodnik
sights atrakcje turystyczne
sightseeing tour wycieczka po mieście
sign znak
silk jedwab
silver srebro
singer pieśniarz
single sam
single room pokój jednoosobowy
single ticket bilet w jedną stronę
sink zlew
sir pan
sister siostra
sit siadać
size rozmiar
skate łyżwa
skewer rożen
ski narta
ski boot but narciarski
ski pole kijek
skin skóra
skirt spódnica
sleep spać
sleeper car [BE] wagon sypialny

sleeping bag śpiwór
sleeping car wagon sypialny
sleeping pill tabletka nasenna
sleeve rękaw
slice plasterek
slip v poślizgnąć się
slipper pantofel
slow wolny
slowly wolno
small mały
smell pachnieć
smoke palić
smoking (area) dla palących
snack przekąska
snack bar bar
sneaker tenisówka
snorkel fajka do nurkowania
snow śnieg
soap mydło
soccer piłka nożna
sock skarpetka
socket gniazdko
sole (shoes) podeszwa
some jakiś
something coś
sometimes czasami
somewhere gdzieś
son syn
soon niedługo
sore throat ból gardła
sorry przepraszam

soul (music) soul
sour kwaśne
south południe
souvenir pamiątka
souvenir store sklep z pamiątkami
spa spa
space miejsce
spare zapasowy
speak mówić
special specjalny
specialist specjalista
specimen próbka
spell v przeliterować
spend (time) spędzać; **(money)** wydawać
spicy ostry
sponge gąbka
spoon łyżka
sport sport
sporting goods store sklep sportowy
spot (place, site) miejsce
sprained skręcony
spring wiosna
square kwadrat
stadium stadion
staff personel
stain plama
stainless steel stal nierdzewna
stairs schody

stamp (postal) znaczek
standby ticket tani bilet okazyjny
start v **(begin)** zaczynać się; **(car)** zapalić
starter [BE] przekąska
statement (police) zeznanie
stationery store sklep papierniczy
statue pomnik
stay n pobyt; v zostać; **(in a hotel)** zatrzymać się
sterilizing solution płyn do sterylizacji
still adv wciąż
stockings [BE] pończochy
stolen ukradziony
stomach brzuch
stomachache ból brzucha
stop n **(bus, tram)** przystanek; v zatrzymywać się
store sklep
store guide tablica informacyjna
storm burza
stove kuchenka
strange dziwny
straw (drinking) słomka
stream strumień
strong (powerful) silny
student student
study v studiować
style styl

subtitled z napisami
suggest zasugerować
suit (men's) garnitur; **(women's)** kostium
suitable stosowny
suitcase walizka
summer lato
sunbathe opalać się
sunburn oparzenie słoneczne
sunglasses okulary słoneczne
sunny słoneczny
sunshade parasol
sunstroke udar słoneczny
suntan lotion krem do opalania
superb znakomity
supermarket supermarket
supervision nadzór
supplement opłata dodatkowa
suppository czopek
sure pewien
surfboard deska do serfowania
surname nazwisko
sweater sweter
sweatshirt bluza
sweet (taste) słodki
swelling opuchlizna
swim pływać
swimming pool basen
swimming trunks kąpielówki
swimsuit kostium kąpielowy
swollen spuchnięty

symptom (illness) objaw
synagogue synagoga

T

table stolik
take brać; **(carry)** zanieść; **(medicine)** brać; **(time)** trwać
take away [BE] na wynos
talk rozmawiać
tall wysoki
tampon tampon
tan opalenizna
tap [BE] kran
tapestry kilim
taxi taksówka
taxi rank [BE] postój taksówek
taxi stand postój taksówek
teacher nauczyciel
team drużyna
teaspoon łyżeczka do herbaty
teddy bear miś
telephone n telefon; v dzwonić
telephone bill rachunek telefoniczny
telephone booth budka telefoniczna
telephone call rozmowa telefoniczna
telephone number numer telefonu
tell powiedzieć

temperature temperatura
temple świątynia
temporarily tymczasowo
tennis tenis
tennis court kort tenisowy
tent namiot
tent peg kołek
tent pole maszt namiotowy
terminal terminal
terrace taras
terrible okropny
terrific wspaniały
tetanus tężec
text *n* **(phone)** sms; **(document)** tekst
thank *v* dziękować
thank you dziękuję
that to
theater teatr
theft kradzież
their(s) ich
theme park tematyczny park rozrywki
then (time) wtedy
there tam
thermometer termometr
these ci
they oni
thick gruby
thief złodziej
thigh udo

thin chudy
think myśleć
thirsty spragniony
this (one) ten
those tamci
thousand tysiąc
throat gardło
through przez
thumb kciuk
ticket bilet
ticket office kasa biletowa
tie krawat
tight *adv* ciasny
tights (clothing) rajstopy
time czas; **(exact time)** godzina
timetable [BE] rozkład jazdy
tin opener [BE] otwieracz do puszek
tire (car) opona
tired zmęczony
tissue chusteczka
to do
tobacco tytoń
tobacconist sklep tytoniowy
today dzisiaj
toe palec u nogi
toilet [BE] toaleta
toilet paper papier toaletowy
tomorrow jutro
tongue język
tonight dziś wieczorem
too (extreme) za

tooth ząb
toothache ból zęba
toothbrush szczoteczka do zębów
toothpaste pasta do zębów
top (head) góra
torn naderwany
tour wycieczka
tour guide przewodnik wycieczki
tour operator organizator wycieczki
tourist turysta
tourist office biuro informacji turystycznej
tow truck pomoc drogowa
towel ręcznik
tower wieża
town miasto
town center centrum
town hall ratusz
toy zabawka
track tor
traditional tradycyjny
traffic ruch
traffic jam korek
traffic light światła
traffic violation wykroczenie drogowe
trailer przyczepa
train pociąg
train station dworzec kolejowy
trained wykwalifikowany

tram tramwaj
transit (travel) przejazd
translate tłumaczyć
translation tłumaczenie
translator tłumacz
trash (garbage) śmieci
trash can śmietnik
travel n podróż; v podróżować
travel agency biuro podróży
travelers check czek podróżny
travelers cheque [BE] czek podróżny
tray taca
tree drzewo
trim v podstrzyc
trip wycieczka
trolley wózek
trousers spodnie
truck ciężarówka
true prawdziwy
try próbować
try on (clothes) przymierzyć
T-shirt t-shirt
tumor nowotwór
tunnel tunel
turn skręcić
turn down zmniejszyć
turn off wyłączyć
turn on włączyć
turn up (volume, heat) zwiększyć

TV telewizor
tweezers pinceta
twice dwa razy
twin bed łóżko podwójne
twist *v* **(hurt)** skręcić
type (sort) rodzaj
typical typowy
tyre [BE] opona

U

U.K. Wielka Brytania
U.S. Stany Zjednoczone
ugly brzydki
ulcer wrzód
umbrella parasol
uncle wuj
uncomfortable niewygodny
unconscious nieprzytomny
under pod
understand rozumieć
underwear bielizna
undress rozbierać (się)
uneven (ground) nierówny
unfortunately niestety
uniform mundur
unit (phone card) impuls
university uniwersytet
unleaded (gas) bezołowiowa
unlimited mileage bez limitu
  kilometrów
unlock otworzyć

unpleasant niemiły
unscrew odkręcić
urgent pilny

V

vacation wakacje
vacuum cleaner odkurzacz
vegetarian *adj* wegetariański; *n*
  wegetarianin
visa wiza

W

wait czekać
wallet portfel
water woda
week tydzień
where gdzie
white biały
window okno
window seat siedzenie przy
  oknie
wine list lista win
wireless bezprzewodowy
work *v* **(function)** działać; **(job)**
  pracować

X

X-ray rentgen

A

aktualny up-to-date
alarm przeciwpożarowy fire alarm
aleja boulevard
ambasada embassy
angielski English
Anglia England
antyki antiques store
aparat fotograficzny camera
apteka pharmacy
artykuły bezcłowe duty-free goods
aseptyczny antiseptic
astma asthma
atrakcja turystyczna tourist attraction
autokar long-distance bus [coach BE]
autostrada highway [motorway BE]

B

bagaż baggage
bagaż podręczny carry-on [hand luggage BE]
bagno marsh
balkon balcony (theater)
balsam po opalaniu after-sun lotion
bankomat ATM
basen dla dzieci children's pool
basen kryty indoor swimming pool
basen odkryty outdoor swimming pool
benzyna gas [petrol BE]
bez cukru sugar-free
bez tłuszczu fat-free
bezglutenowy gluten-free
bezołowiowy unleaded (gasoline)
bezprzewodowy wireless (internet)
bezzwrotny non-returnable
biblioteka library
biegać v run
biegówki cross-coutry skis
bielizna underwear
bilet ticket
bilet elektroniczny e-ticket
bilet grupowy group ticket
bilet okresowy season ticket
bilet parkingowy parking ticket
biuro office
biuro obsługi klienta customer service
biuro podróży travel agency
biuro rzeczy znalezionych lost-and-found [lost-property office BE]
biuro turystyczne tourist office

biznes business
biżuteria jewelry
błąd mistake
blokada lock (on a bike)
błyszczyk lipgloss
ból pain
budka autobusowa bus shelter
bungalow bungalow
but shoe
butelka bottle

C

cena price
centrum biznesu business district
centrum handlowe shopping mall [centre BE]
centrum miasta downtown area [town centre BE]
centrum odnowy biologicznej spa
centrum ogrodnicze garden center
chemiczna toaleta chemical toilet
chodnik sidewalk [pavement BE]
ciepły warm (water)
ciężarówka truck
ciężki heavy (luggage)
cło duty (customs)
cmentarz cemetery
cukiernia pastry shop
czasopismo magazine
czek check [cheque BE]
czek podróżny travelers check [cheque BE]
czekać wait

D

dabingowany dubbed
dania dnia menu of the day
darowizna donation
data urodzenia date of birth
data ważności expiration [expiry BE] date
dawkowanie dosage
deklaracja celna customs declaration
delikatesy delicatessen
deska do windsurfingu windsurfing board
deska surfingowa surfboard
dieta diet
długopis pen
do until
do wynajęcia for rent [hire BE]
do żucia chewable (tablets)
dokładna reszta exact change
dom mieszkalny apartment buildin
dom towarowy department store
domowej roboty homemade
dostawa delivery
dostęp access
dowód tożsamości identification
dozorca caretaker
drewno wood

droga road
drzewo tree
drzwi automatyczne automatic doors
drzwi przeciwpożarowe fire door
dworzec autobusowy bus station
dworzec kolejowy train station
dzbanek pot (for tea)
działać v work
działanie uboczne side effect
dziecko child
dzień day
dzień powszedni weekday
dzisiaj today

E

e-mail e-mail
emeryt senior citizen
epilepsja epilepsy
epileptyk epileptic

F

fabryka factory
fajerwerk firework
faks fax
festyn fair
filharmonia concert hall
filiżanka cup
folia aluminiowa aluminum [kitchen BE] foil
formularz form

fotelik dziecięcy car seat
fryzjer hairdresser
funt pound (sterling)

G

gabinet dentystyczny dental office [surgery BE]
gabinet lekarski doctor's office [surgery BE]
galeria gallery
garnek pot (for cooking)
gaśnica fire extinguisher
gdzie where
giełda stock exchange
głęboko deep
godzina hour
godziny urzędowania business hours
godziny wizyt visiting hours
góra mountain
gorączka temperature
gość guest
gospodarstwo farm
gotować v boil
gotówka cash

H

hala targowa indoor market
hamulec bezpieczeństwa emergency brake
hasło password

I

ile how many, how much

imię name

informacja information desk

informacja dla klientów customer information

informacja o lotach flight information

informacja o sklepie store directory [guide BE]

instruktor instructor

internet internet

izba przyjęć emergency ward

J

jadalnia dining room

jakość quality

jaskinia cave

jasny light (color)

jeden one

jedwab silk

jedzenie na wynos to go [takeaway BE] (food)

jesień fall [autumn BE]

jeść eat

jezioro lake

jeździectwo horseback riding

język tongue (part of body); language

język obcy foreign language

jubiler jeweler

jutro tomorrow

K

kafejka internetowa internet cafe

kamizelka ratunkowa life jacket

kantor currency exchange office

kapliczka shrine

kapsułka capsule (medication)

karetka ambulance

karta key card (hotel)

karta do telefonu phone card

karta kredytowa credit card

karta pokładowa boarding pass (airport)

karta rabatowa discount card

karta win wine list

kasa biletowa ticket office

kasa ekspresowa express checkout

kasjer cashier

kask crash helmet

katedra cathedral

kaucja deposit

kawałek piece

klieliszek glass (alcoholic)

kierownik manager

kierunek direction (map)

kilometr kilometer

kiosk z gazetami newsstand

klasa biznes business class

klasa turystyczna economy class

klif cliff
klimatyzacja air conditioning
klimatyzator air conditioner
klinika clinic
kolejka linowa cable car
koło ratunkowe life preserver [belt BE]
komiks comic book
komisariat police station
kompresor air pump (gas station)
komputer computer
koncert concert
konkurs contest
kontaktować v contact
kontrola celna customs control
kontroler biletów ticket inspector
korek traffic jam
kościół church
kosmetyki cosmetics
koszerny kosher
kosztować v cost
koszyk shopping basket
kradzież theft
krajowy domestic (flight)
kran faucet [tap BE]
krem nawilżający moisturizer
krem z blokadą UV sunscreen
kropla drop (medication)
krwotok bleeding
książka telefoniczna directory
księgarnia bookstore

kucharz cook, chef
kuchenka mikrofalowa microwave
kuchnia kitchen
kurs wymiany exchange rate
kuszetka berth (train)
kwiaciarnia florist
kwiat flower
kwota amount (money)

L

lądować arrive (plane)
las forest
latarnia morska lighthouse
lato summer
lecieć v fly
lekarz doctor
lekki light (weight)
leżak deck chair
linia (lotnicza) airline
list polecony registered letter
list priorytetowy express mail
lista drinków drink menu
lokalny local
lot flight
loteria lottery
lotnisko airport
lotnisko krajowe domestic airport
lotnisko międzynarodowe international airport
lubić v like

Ł

łazienka bathroom
łopatka spatula
łódź ratunkowa life boat
łóżeczko dziecięce crib [child's cot *BE*]
łóżko bed
łyżka do odmierzania measuring spoon
łyżwiarstwo ice skating
łyżwy ice skates

M

mały small (size)
mapa drogowa road map
matka mother
mdłości nausea
mdły bland
meble furniture
mgła fog
miarka kuchenna measuring cup
miejsce seat (bus, train, plane)
miejsce na piknik picnic area
miejsce przy oknie window seat
miejsce przy przejściu aisle seat
miejsce urodzenia place of birth
miejsce zbiórki meeting place [point *BE*]
miejscówka reservation (train)
międzynarodowy international
mikrofalówka mircowave

miska bowl
mleczarnia dairy
młodzież youth
młyn windmill
mniej less
moczary swamp
mokry wet
mop mop
morze sea
motor motorcycle
motorower moped
mówić speak
msza mass
muzeum museum
mydło soap

N

na dole downstairs
na górze upstairs
na zewnątrz outside
nadbagaż excess baggage
namiot tent
napad mugging
napisać write
napiwek tip
naprawa *n* repair (car)
naprawić *v* fix (a car)
narty wodne water skis
następny next
nawierzchnia road surface
nawilżacz moisturizer

nazwisko last name
nazwisko panieńskie maiden
  name
niedaleko close
niepalący non-smoking
nierówny uneven (surface)
noc night
nocleg accommodation
nocny dyżur night duty
nocny portier night porter
normalny normal
nowy new
numer kierunkowy country code
numer lotu flight number
numer miejsca seat number
numer pierwszej pomocy
  emergency number

O

objazd detour [diversion *BE*]
obóz *n* camp
obozować *v* camp
od from (time)
odbiór bagażu baggage claim
oddział department
odebrać receive
odkurzacz vacuum cleaner
odlatywać leave
odprawa check-in (airport)
odprawa bagażu baggage check
odwołany cancelled

odzież damska ladieswear
odzież męska menswear
ognisko campfire
ograniczenie prędkości speed
  limit
ogród garden
okazja bargain
okno window
okres period (of time);
  menstruation
okulary glasses (optical)
okulary przeciwsłoneczne
  sunglasses
opera opera
opis description
opłata bankowa bank charge
opłata obowiązkowa minimum
  charge
opłata za dzień day charge
opłata za usługę service charge
opłata za wstęp admission charge
opóźniony delayed
optyk optician
ostry spicy
ostrzeżenie warning
otwarty open (shop)

P

paczka package [parcel *BE*]
paczka ekspresowa express mail
pakować pack

palacz smoker
paliwo fuel
pan sir
pani madam
panie ladies (toilet)
panna miss
panowie gentlemen (toilet)
papierowy ręcznik paper towel
paragon receipt
parasol umbrella [sunshade BE]
park narodowy national park
park publiczny public park
parking parking lot [car park BE]
parking podziemny underground garage
parking wielopoziomowy parking garage
parkometr parking meter
parkować v park
parter first floor [ground floor BE]; orchestra [stalls BE] (theater)
pas lane
pasażer passenger
pasmo górskie mountain range
pawilon pavilion
pchać push
pchli targ flea market
peron platform
piasek sand
pić v drink
piekarnia bakery

pielęgniarka nurse
pieniądze money
pierwsza klasa first class
pierwsza pomoc emergency services; first aid
pierwsze piętro second floor [first floor BE]
pieszy pedestrian
piętro floor (level in building)
pigułka pill
pikantny spicy
pilny urgent
pismo periodical
piwnica basement
plac square
plasterek slice
plaża dla nudystów nudist beach
plecak backpack
plomba filling (dental)
płacić v pay
płeć sex (gender)
płyta kompaktowa CD
płytki adj shallow
pływać v swim
po południu p.m.
pociąg Intercity Intercity train
pociąg lokalny local train
początkujący beginner
poczekalnia waiting room
poczta post office

podarunek gift
podjazd ramp
podłoga floor
podobać się like
podpaska sanitary napkin [pad *BE*]
podróż powrotna round-trip [return trip *BE*] (ticket)
poduszka pillow
pokład deck (ship)
pokoje do wynajęcia rooms for rent [to let *BE*]
pokój room (hotel)
pole field
pole bitwy battle site
pole namiotowe camping
polecać recommend
policja police
policja drogowa traffic police
polisa ubezpieczeniowa insurance card [certificate *BE*]
Polska Poland
południe noon (time); south (direction)
pomiędzy between
pomnik monument
pomoc drogowa breakdown services
poranek morning
port port
portfel wallet
postój taksówek taxi stand [rank

BE]
pościel sheets
potrzebny required
potwierdzenie confirmation
potwierdzić confirm
powiedzieć *v* say
powtórzyć repeat
poznać meet
pożar fire
północ midnight (time); north (direction)
półwysep peninsula
pracować *v* work
prać oddzielnie wash separately
prać ręcznie hand wash only
pralnia laundry
pralnia chemiczna dry-cleaner
prasować *v* iron
prawnik lawyer
prawo jazdy driver's license
priorytet express mail
progi rzeczne rapids
prognoza pogody weather forecast
prom ferry
proszę please
prowizja commission
prysznic shower
prywatny private
przebieralnia fitting room
przecena sale

przechowalnia bagażu baggage office

przeciek leak

przed before

przed południem a.m.

przedstawić introduce (someone)

przedział compartment

przejście path; aisle (plane)

przejście dla pieszych pedestrian crossing

przejście podziemne underpass

przejściówka adapter

przekaz pieniężny money order

przekąska appetizer [starter *BE*]

przepaść precipice

przepychacz plunger

przesiadać się change [transfer *BE*] (bus)

przesyłka package

przeszkadzać disturb

przetłumaczyć translate

przewodnik guide (person); guidebook

przyczepa trailer

przyloty arrivals (airport)

przymierzalnia fitting room

przystanek autobusowy bus stop

przystanek na żądanie on-demand stop

ptak bird

punkt widzenia view point

pusty vacant

R

rabat discount

ratownik lifeguard

ratusz town hall

recepta prescription

recycling recycling

ręcznie robione handmade

ręcznik towel

rejs cruise

reklama advertisment

rentgen X-ray

restauracja restaurant

reszta *n* change (money)

rezerwacja reservation

rezerwuar reservoir

robak bug

rogatka toll booth

rondel saucepan

rondo roundabout

room service room service

rower bicycle

rozkład jazdy schedule [timetable *BE*]

rozkładane łóżko cot

rozmowa na koszt rozmówcy collect call [reverse-charge call *BE*]

rozumieć understand

rura pipe (water)

rząd row (of seats, people)
rzeka river
rzeźnik butcher

S

sąd courthouse
sala hall (large public room)
sala konferencyjna conference room
sala zebrań convention hall
salon gier arcade
sam alone
samolot plane
sauna sauna
schowek na bagaż luggage locker
schronisko młodzieżowe youth hostel
ściana wall
ścieżka path
sekretarka secretary
serwetka napkin
sieć network (of computers); chain (of stores)
siedzenie seat
siedzenie przy korytarzu aisle seat
siedzenie przy oknie window seat
silnik engine
siłownia gym
skala scale
skała rock
skasować validate (ticket)

skipass ski pass
sklep store
sklep bezcłowy duty-free store
sklep mięsny butcher shop
sklep muzyczny music store
sklep osiedlowy convenience store
sklep papierniczy stationery store
sklep z narzędziami hardware store
sklep z zabawkami toy store
sklep ze zdrową żywnością health food store
skóra leather; skin
skręcić *v* turn
skrytka bagażowa luggage locker
skrzynka pocztowa mailbox [postbox *BE*]
skrzyżowanie intersection [junction *BE*]
skuter wodny jet-ski
ślepy zaułek dead end
śliski slippery
słony salty
śmieci trash [rubbish *BE*]
śniadanie breakfast
spa spa
śpiący policjant speed bump
spotkanie appointment (business); meeting (friends)
spóźniony late
stacja benzynowa gas [petrol *BE*] station

stacja kolejowa train [railway *BE*] station

stadion stadium

stal steel

stanowisko odprawy check-in desk (airport)

Stany Zjednoczone United States

startować take off, depart

statek ship

staw pond

steward flight attendant

stój codzienny casual clothing

stolik table

straż pożarna fire station

strażak firefighter

strój suit, clothing

strój wieczorowy evening dress

strój wizytowy formal dress

strumień stream

studiować *v* study

suszarka do włosów hairdryer

światła traffic light

światło light

święto państwowe national holiday

świeży fresh

szewc shoe repair [cobbler *BE*]

szklanka glass (non-alcoholic)

szkoła school

szlak trail

szpital hospital

T

tabletka tablet

taksówka taxi

talerz plate

targ market

telefon phone

telefon komórkowy cell phone [mobile phone *BE*]

telefon publiczny pay phone

telefonistka operator (phone)

terminal terminal

toaleta restroom [toilet *BE*]

tor track [platform *BE*]

tor wyścigowy racetrack [race course *BE*]

torebka purse [handbag *BE*]

trampolina diving board

trasa route

trasa autobusowa bus route

trawa grass

turystyka piesza hiking

tutaj here

tydzień week

tylko only

U

ubezpieczenie insurance

ugryzienie bite

ulepszony improved

ulica street

ulica jednokierunkowa one-way

street
uniwersytet university
unowocześniony modernized
usługa service
uwaga attention

W

w budowie under construction
w jedną stronę one-way (trip)
wagon car (train)
wagon restauracyjny dining car (train)
wakacyjny rozkład jazdy holiday schedule [timetable *BE*]
walizka suitcase
waluta obca foreign currency
warsztat samochodowy car mechanic [repair garage *BE*]
wąwóz gorge
wejście entrance; gate (at the airport)
wełna wool
wentylator fan (electric)
wesołe miasteczko amusement park
wewnętrzny extension (phone)
wiadomość news
widelec fork
więcej more
Wielka Brytania Great Britain
wieczór evening
wiedza knowledge
winda elevator [lift *BE*]

windsurfing windsurfing
wiosna spring
włączyć turn on
własność prywatna private property
woda water
wolno slowly
wolny free (place)
wolny pokój vacancy (accommodation)
wózek bagażowy luggage cart [trolley *BE*]
wpłata deposit
wschód east
wskazówka instruction
wspinaczka rock climbing
wstęp wolny admission free
wstęp wzbroniony no access
wybrzeże coast
wydarzenie event
wydrukować *v* print
wyjście exit; gate (at the airport)
wyjście bezpieczeństwa emergency exit
wyjście przeciwpożarowe fire exit
wyjście wzbronione no exit
wykręcić dial
wyłączyć turn off
wylogować się log off
wymiana exchange
wymiana walut currency exchange
wynajem samochodów car rental

[hire *BE*]
wypadek accident
wypłata cash withdrawal
wyprzedaż clearance
wyprzedzać *v* pass (car)
wysiąść get off (bus, train)
wysłać send
wysokie krzesełko highchair
występ show (in front of audience)
wzbroniony forbidden
wzgórze hill

Z

z napisami subtitled
zaawansowany advanced
zabawka toy
zachód west
zaczekać wait
zadzwonić call (phone)
zagraniczny international (flight);
  foreign (product)
zajazd guest house
zakaźny contagious, infectious
zakupy shopping
zalogować się log on
zamawiać *v* order
zamek castle (building); lock (door)
zamknięty closed (store)
zamówienie *n* order
zamrożony frozen
zamykać *v* lock

zapakować wrap
zapakować na prezent giftwrap
zaparcie constipation
zapinać fasten (seat belt)
zapłacony paid
zapominać forget
zarezerwować reserve (tickets)
zatkany blocked
zatłoczony crowded
zatoka bay
zatrzymać się stay (at a hotel); stop
  (not move)
zebra pedestrian crossing
zepsuty broken
zgwałcić *v* rape
zima winter
zimno *adv* cold
zimny *adj* cold
złoto gold
zły bad
znaczek stamp
znaczek pocztowy postage stamp
znaczyć mean (meaning)
znak drogowy road sign
zniżka discount
zwolnić slow down
zwrot pieniędzy refund
zwrotny returnable

Ż

żelazko *n* iron